Authenticity, Passion, and Advocacy

"Seeking to understand how Catholic teaching is received by the modern adolescent, Dr. Thomas Malewitz presents a path of formation for those who teach and form adolescents, with the Trappist monk Thomas Merton as a guide and model . . . Dr. Malewitz includes Merton's letters and communication with adolescents, which illustrate Merton's ability to listen, enter into dialogue, and communicate an understanding of the true self always seeking God. This is a must-read for the minister who seeks to form well the adolescents entrusted to his or her care."

—**JOSEPH E. KURTZ**
Archbishop of Louisville

"Writing from many years of hands-on experience in the classroom, along with his profound reading of Merton, Thomas Malewitz provides an excellent roadmap for Christian educators to incorporate, indeed immerse, their adolescent curricula in the timeless and prescient wisdom of Thomas Merton."

—**PAUL M. PEARSON**
Director, Thomas Merton Center

"This is a wonderful text for all educators interested in supporting adolescents in developing their spiritual, ethical, and discerning selves—to help them understand their particular place in the world as a positive force for change and the cultivation of happiness. It's a text that is clearly needed today. Malewitz does a superb job of weaving together theory, practical ideas, and student voice. It's a text for educators to revisit time and again."

—**ELIZABETH G. DINKINS**
Dean, Annsley Frazier Thornton
School of Education, Bellarmine University

"As an orphan and mildly misguided adolescent, Thomas Merton had to find his own reliable mentors before eventually becoming a powerful guide for others. Through this careful and fascinating study of Merton's encounters with young people, Tom Malewitz has expertly constructed an insightful and practical resource that will be treasured by teachers, youth ministers, parents, and mentors."

—**JOSEPH Q. RAAB**
Co-Editor of The Merton Annual: Studies in Culture,
Spirituality, and Social Concerns

"Thomas Malewitz reminds us that the adolescent journey of self-discovery is an encounter with the sacred. Through his own research, reflections, and experiences as a high school theology teacher, Dr. Malewitz has successfully bridged the interactive, contemplative world of Thomas Merton with twenty-first-century adolescent spirituality, creating a unique perspective on the formation and education of young people."

—**ARTHUR L. TURNER**
Director for the Office of Faith Formation,
Archdiocese of Louisville

Authenticity, Passion, and Advocacy

Approaching Adolescent Spirituality from the Life
and Wisdom of Thomas Merton

Thomas E. Malewitz

Foreword by Thomas Del Prete

WIPF & STOCK · Eugene, Oregon

AUTHENTICITY, PASSION, AND ADVOCACY
Approaching Adolescent Spirituality from the Life and Wisdom of Thomas Merton

Wipf & Stock
An Imprint of Wipf and Stock Publishers
199 W. 8th Ave., Suite 3
Eugene, OR 97401

www.wipfandstock.com

PAPERBACK ISBN: 978-1-5326-8222-3
HARDCOVER ISBN: 978-1-5326-8223-0
EBOOK ISBN: 978-1-5326-8224-7

Manufactured in the U.S.A.   06/25/20

To
Bridget
Meredith, Brenna, and Hope:
Inspiration and blessing begin within the family.

What can we gain by sailing to the moon if we are not able to cross the abyss that separates us from ourselves?

—THOMAS MERTON, *THE WISDOM OF THE DESERT.*

Contents

Images

Chapter 1. Introduction

Chapter 2. Thomas Merton

Chapter 3. Education

Chapter 4. Rituals

Chapter 5. Silence

Chapter 6. True/False Self

Chapter 7. Passion

Chapter 8. Athletics

Chapter 9. The Arts, Pt. I—Music/Poetry

Chapter 10. The Arts, Pt. II—Painting/Photography

Chapter 11. Advocacy

Foreword

A WELL-KNOWN PRAYER WRITTEN by Thomas Merton begins, "My Lord God, I have no idea where I am going. I do not see the road ahead of me. I cannot know for certain where it will end. Nor do I really know myself."[1] As much as Merton's words might resonate with any of us, they would seem to be particularly powerful for young people. For it is young people who perhaps feel most acutely the uncertainties of life—of who they are and where they are going, of who others are and the society they live in and create together. It naturally follows that young people might appreciate guideposts from someone like Merton. That is to say, they might appreciate the honesty of someone who acknowledges uncertainty frankly; who eschews facile claims and false assurances; who can affirm the challenge of finding the road ahead; who shares their secret hope to learn something real and true about themselves and others, to find a spiritual ground for their life journeys.

The search for self and meaning can make us susceptible to ways of being and doing that offer the promise of certainty, but which in fact are superficial, which endorse what Merton often called the psychological or false self. There is seemingly an inexhaustible source of allure, especially on the internet. Love itself is represented in a welter of commodified forms. Who you are can be defined and redefined in multiple ways through social media and the attendant power to image oneself variously. The internet itself can be mistaken as a source of identity.

Better, Merton would say, to find ourselves more deeply. Better to cultivate our inner selves even while establishing ourselves socially and culturally. Better to discover ourselves by discovering the humanity of others, by learning what is uniquely ours to give with love to the world, and by

1. Merton, *Thoughts in Solitude*, 83.

learning to form genuine communities. As he wrote to friends within a few months of his accidental death, "Our real journey in life is interior: It is a matter of growth, deepening, and of an even greater surrender to the action of love and grace in our hearts."[2]

If young people feel uncertainty deeply, they also remind us about hope, possibility, the sheer exuberance of life. Here again, Merton can be helpful. If the inner journey is about realizing the availability and power of love in all of us, is about finding ourselves and others in this love, it means also, paradoxically, an opening outward, an ever-deepening affirmation of life. Merton's inner journey led him to rediscover and deepen his relationship with the world in multiple life—affirming ways. Young people today would be drawn to many of his concerns and interests—social justice; ecological wholeness; nonviolence; intercultural, interreligious, and cross-cultural communication; authentic voice in music, poetry, and literature; the impact of mass communication; the power of visual, especially photographic images; human-relatedness; and, not least, the intuition and experience of the presence of God and God's love in life. They might be drawn to his artistic affirmation of life and God's presence, as expressed especially in his poetry, calligraphies, and photography, but also in his appreciation for music and the life that pulses through it (he was a jazz aficionado, playing the latest John Coltrane on the record player he had at his hermitage in the mid-1960s, but also Bob Dylan and the Beatles).

What distinguishes Merton is the extent to which his Christian contemplative life, centered on awareness of and attentiveness to the presence of God, animated and guided his social, ecological, artistic, and human concerns. Contemplation and spirituality might seem anachronistic to some young people, or a recipe for remoteness, isolation, and disconnection. But Merton's example says otherwise. His contemplative life helped him become more fully his whole real self, more fully awake, attuned, and alive. It nurtured a deep understanding of his relatedness to others in "the hidden ground of love." It formed his resolution to speak out against war, against racism, and in solidarity on behalf of those suffering from human injustice. His journey shows how spirituality, self, and life are hardly separate—as if spirituality is only what happens in a monastery or in a church—but rather intimately related and relevant. As he wrote to James Forest, at the time a young activist peacemaker, "the great thing" is not to look for an identity in the efficacy of one's action, but to live and to learn

2. Merton, "September 1968 Circular Letter to Friends," 296.

to be "used by God's love."[3] Merton's example can open young people to the power of a spirituality and love that affirm them deeply, that tap into their hope and desire for an authentic and meaningful life; can help them in their formation as whole persons.

Within these pages you will find a curriculum that uses Merton as a guide and resource for awakening the spiritual lives of young people, and for helping them to discover themselves more fully as they navigate the terrain of their own life journeys. Merton's spiritual journey and interests are explained to give context for the curricular themes, which in turn are aligned with themes emerging from the National Study of Youth and Religion. Concepts such as ritual, silence, authenticity, passion, and discipline punctuate the curriculum. Informed by Catholic tradition and Mertonian insight, the curriculum at the same time is attuned to the importance of experience and reflection in fostering learning meant to support the process of discovering oneself more fully. Through the curriculum, young people have an opportunity to learn experientially through practices such as meditation and to reflect on the story of Merton and others, including stories captured in film and literature. Young people have an opportunity to revisit familiar pursuits, such as sports, music, the arts, painting, and photography, in ways that explore their relation to their deeper selves. Finally, students visit anew their social lives and how they are carried out, with themes of bullying, relationship, inclusion, and advocacy, as well as community-building, all addressed.

There is a parallel curriculum in the book, one that calls us in our vocation as educators to reflect on ourselves and our practice, one that orients us to a pedagogy based on humility, trust, respect, and support for young people in their development as whole persons in their current social context. Engaging this book is an opportunity to think afresh about how to help young people open to a greater understanding of themselves and their capacities for love, silence, creative expression, meaningful social action, and community-building.

Thomas Del Prete, EdD
Professor of Practice, Clark University
Director of the Adam Institute
for Urban Teaching and School Practice

3. Merton, "Letter to James Forest, February 21, 1966," 291.

Preface

WHILE WRITING THIS BOOK, I have come to a much greater awareness of the challenge and complexity of addressing adolescent spirituality. Much like in the lives of adolescents, there is no one repeated experience; each human being is unique and that authenticity offers beauty within the world. I hope that the reader will approach this book as an exploration of themes that relate to contemporary adolescent spirituality while appreciating that the contents within will not offer all of the answers to resolve every challenge that arises with adolescents.

I can attest as a stepfather of three teenage daughters, a full-time high school theology educator at a Catholic all-boys high school, as well as previous experience as a director of religious education and director of youth ministry, I do not have it all together. Some days with adolescents go well, and some do not. I think that is why I found inspiration in the life and writings of Thomas Merton, the spiritual seeker and mystic. I take great comfort in Merton's desire for wholeness and holiness, not through an unattainable perfection but through the search of the authenticity found within living the life we were created for.

Roots of the Topic

The topic for this manuscript evolved primarily from my dissertation research which explored implementing a curriculum to respond to the epidemic of adolescent bullying, based on themes from the writing of Thomas Merton. The dissertation was a qualitative study and was founded upon the creation and pilot implementation of the curriculum within a class of high school freshmen theology students. Twenty-three freshmen students, academically identified at the honors level, from an all-male Midwest urban

Catholic school were invited to participate in the study. From the initial twenty-three students; sixteen students returned the completed parental and student consent form to participate in the study. The first-iteration curriculum was implemented over the course of ten nonconsecutive school days where the class periods during the implementation ranged from thirty minutes to forty-five minutes long. The curriculum activities did not include a grade for the students participating in the study.

Seventy-one unique student artifacts were collected over the initial implementation. These artifacts ranged from page-length essays to simple bullet points depending on the topic and activity. In the role of researcher, I also took down fieldnotes throughout the course of the implementation. To supplement the fieldnotes, I would return in the evening to watch and listen to the recorded files and jot down further notations that were overlooked during the implementation experience earlier in the day. Follow-up questions were also conducted to clarify student responses when warranted.

Video recordings of the student dialogues were also taken to help capture active aspects of the student—participant tone, inflections, and body language missed from fieldnotes alone. These recordings also helped as a recorded cross-reference to the written experiences of the students during oral dialoguing. A total of two hours and thirty-seven minutes of recorded student dialogue and activity was collected and were personally transcribed by the researcher for the study. Throughout the transcription process, the audio comments were identified for each student, labeling them by their initials, as well as making notes of observational data of student posture and tone. As was stated in the consent form, after the transcription of the data, the video-recording files were deleted to ensure student confidentiality.

Throughout the transcription and coding process of the data, thematic similarities and patterns emerged from the transcribed conversations and collect artificats. These emergent themes will be discussed at different points throughout this manuscript. Likewise, some of the collected student data will be explored within a topical context as evidence of trends of adolescent thought and behavior. For additional information about the curriculum or specific information regarding the qualitative methodology used within the study, see the complete dissertation study, which can be found online through Bellarmine University.[1]

---

1. See: Malewitz, *"No One is an Island."*

For the Reader

This text, although derived from my dissertation, expands upon that original study. To help establish the importance of the chosen themes in the life of adolescents, I have attempted to include aspects that weave together both theory and practical application for the reader. Chapters 1 and 2 serve as an introduction to the two main premises of the manuscript: adolescent spirituality and Thomas Merton. The remaining chapters relating to adolescent spirituality each explore the given topical theme through the following chapter sections:

1. An introductory quote from the writings of Thomas Merton, with a brief contextual explanation

2. A direct connection between the topic and adolescence

3. Experiences that bridge the writings of Thomas Merton to the topic

4. The inclusion of either direct data from adolescents regarding the topic or a section that offers direct application of the topic with adolescents

5. A few concluding practical questions for personal examination.

Invitation to Explore Merton's Insights of Adolescent Spirituality

Throughout my research of Merton's writings, I became intrigued with his communication with adolescents and his keen awareness about the spiritual needs and development of those adolescents. It should not be underestimated how aware Thomas Merton was of the world around him, even though he was a monk and hermit. He had a pulse on the signs of the times; not just his times but also a deep knowledge of the essence of the human experience. As you will see through this book, his writings offer insightful guidance for unanticipated challenges of the twenty-first century. Although there is precious little that directly connects Thomas Merton with adolescents, there is much to examine about the words that remain as an example of a prophet ahead his time. I hope that this manuscript will inspire you to explore the writings of Thomas Merton and see what further wellsprings might emerge.

As a final note, much like the expansive mind and writings of Thomas Merton, this text includes scholarly research, a pastoral context, and practical components. Thomas Merton was a man of a multitude of interests, a continual learner and expansive thinker—although this may seem off-putting from a purely systematic lens, a strictly moral puritan lens, or a sheltered thinker I think it was his expansive nature of inquiry that allowed Merton to understand the challenges of humanity at its deepest and most authentic core. It is important to recognize that all three aspects, scholarship, pastoral context, and practice, also help offer a more complete lens to the complexity of an approach to engage adolescent spirituality. I hope that you will find each of these components helpful as you read the text and that they will offer further resources in your life and ministry.

Acknowledgements

THE CULMINATION OF THIS manuscript has come together through the time, effort, and sacrifice of a community of many extraordinary individuals. I would like to extend my appreciation especially to Dr. Thomas Del Prete, who not only generously wrote the foreword for this manuscript, but whose research into the pedagogical approach of Thomas Merton became the inspiration and catalyst for me to pursue my dissertation research. I am also grateful to Dr. Paul Pearson, director of the Thomas Merton Center, for his time, energy, and continual encouragement throughout the journey of this manuscript; as well as Mark Meade, the assistant director of the Merton Center, as his knowledge of Thomas Merton and response rate to my queries were always punctual and extremely thorough. I am very grateful for their assistance with securing photo permissions and making the included Merton photos available for this manuscript. I am also very grateful for Christopher Wait's work at New Directions for allowing the permissions to include the poetry selections within this manuscript as concrete examples of Thomas Merton's poetic writing. I would like to also extend my gratitude to Matt Wimer at Wipf & Stock for his patience and support throughout the progress of completing my first manuscript.

To my friend and colleague, Beatriz Pacheco, thank you very much for your work with the initial proofreading and editing suggestions. Likewise, to my step-daughter Brenna Lucas for her proofreading and suggestions from a younger generation's point of view. I am very proud and grateful of all of your suggestions and clarity.

Finally, I am most grateful and thankful for the time, support, sacrifice, and love of my wife and stepdaughters throughout this research and writing process without which this manuscript would not have been able to be completed. Thank you all very much.

1

Introduction

Bridging the Gap—Adolescence and Merton

I live alone in the woods and borrowed a record player. I am a real sneaky
hermit and oh yes I love the hippies and am an underground hippy monk but I
don't need LSD to turn on either. The birds turn me on.[1]

AT FACE VALUE, THIS initial quotation may seem like a bizarre and reckless
conversation between a Catholic priest and an adolescent. One could only
imagine what would happen if a cleric today posted a similar response to
an adolescent on Facebook, Twitter, or Instagram. What would the social
media backlash be? What would the trolling comments or accusations
look like? But this brief section of correspondence between Thomas Merton, a Trappist monk, and Suzanne Buturovich, a sixteen-year-old high
school student, can offer insight into the relationship of Merton and the
tangible experience and mindset of one Californian adolescent from the
late 1960s. These passing comments also show that a hermit in Kentucky
was not only well aware of LSD,[2] but also the hippie movement; like an
inquiring adolescent Merton explored the world around him.

1. Merton, "Letter to Suzanne Butorovich, June 22, 1967," 309.

2. Exploring the effects of LSD was a common topic of conversation throughout the
mid-to-late 1960s, especially in California. Acid tests were popularized by Ken Kesey, Neil
Cassady, and other members of the Beat generation throughout 1965 and 1966. Although
LSD was made illegal in California in October 1966, it was still heavily used and promoted

It could be a strange thought that a priest and hermit would have such a pulse on the pop culture of the time. For some people this conversation might lead to a mental image of some type of prophetic-folksy character; like a combination between John the Baptist and a Dylanesque folk-poet who engaged a world in extremes. Clearly Merton illustrated that he was savvy to contemporary trends and contemporary colloquial phrases but he also found a mystical beauty in the natural world. The American 1960s was a time of extreme social behaviors, especially in California: experimentation, free love, and rock-and-roll ruled the minds of the youth culture of that period. A self-proclaimed resistor of television, Merton nonetheless was an artisan, musicophile, and poet who gathered bits of information about the happenings of the world through correspondences, magazines, and friendships.

> I have only watched TV twice in my life. I am frankly not terribly interested in TV anyway. Certainly I do not pretend that by simply refusing to keep up with the latest news I am therefore unaffected by what goes on, or free of it all.[3]

Although a hermit in the rural lands of Kentucky, Merton was not oblivious to the pulse of the culture, nor to the signs of the times affecting his environment.

---

at concerts and through popular musicians like the Grateful Dead and Jefferson Airplane. Thomas Merton was inquisitive and had several letters that referred to the topic of LSD, as he investigated the world that existed around him, as well as offered insight for individuals seeking his guidance. See Merton's correspondence in *The Road to Joy*, such as: with "John" (pp. 327–28) and "Lisa Bieberman," a psychologist whose article on LSD inspired Merton to contact her seeking further information about the drug (pp. 351–52).

3. Merton, *Faith and Violence*, 151.

Introduction

Thomas Merton was no ordinary individual or sheltered hermit. His wisdom bears a deep and penetrating probe into the identity of the human person as well as society. To appreciate the prophetic awareness throughout his writings, a reader cannot reduce Merton's works to the sterile cultural standards of contemporary America; such as is common in the Call-Out or Cancel Culture Movement.[4] The quotation at the beginning of this chapter, beyond the mere words on the page, offers a concrete example that Merton had an innate understanding of the honesty within an adolescent's questions, and through an honest response that might seem off-putting, illustrated God's presence to that young adult.

Before discussing Merton's life and ministry further, it is important to acknowledge the great challenge that exists when exploring the life and personal communications of a deceased celebrity or scholar. Reading the words and writings from an individual's diary or correspondence can often leave an outsider with the feeling of intrusion, a sense of invasion of privacy, especially when a section of text is taken out of original context. Snippets of conversations which bear a clear or profound meaning in the original dialogue can easily become misunderstood or misinterpreted by outsiders. For an author and researcher, questions of establishing integrity, an authentic context, while trying to advance a new perspective and exploration to understand how to apply the life and thought of a celebrated individual can feel like walking a tightrope. This text will attempt to offer such a funambulist insight into the life of Thomas Merton: not only as a monk, celebrated spiritual author, civil-rights advocate, nonviolent resistor, and ecumenical force, but forerunner for insights of a holistic approach to adolescent spirituality.

I also fully acknowledge that during his own lifetime, Thomas Merton was well aware and cautious about his own legacy and celebrated image. In one of his last interviews, Merton referred to this challenge: "The legend is stronger than I am. Nevertheless, I rebel against it and maintain my basic human right not to be turned into a Catholic myth for children

---

4. The Call-Out or Cancel Culture Movement refers to the extreme form of boycotting of a person or event based on an ideological difference. Through this type of boycott, a person or event is canceled or totally removed, isolated, or disregarded from the boycotter's life, communication, or relationships. See Yar and Bromwich, "Tales from the Teenage Cancel Culture" for concrete examples of trends associated with the Cancel Culture Movement.

in parochial schools."[5] Similarly in an essay on education he reflected: "If it so happened that I had once written a best-seller, this was a pure accident, due to inattention and naiveté, and I would take very good care never to do the same again."[6]

The purpose of this manuscript is not to turn Thomas Merton into a Catholic myth, as he feared; it is to acknowledge that the writings of Merton continue to offer wisdom for a culture half-a-century after his death, and most pointedly Merton's life and writings can offer an innate sense of the value of relationship that can shed insight into the challenges for ministry of adolescents, as well as an authentic lens to understand adolescent spirituality.

Adolescent Spirituality: A Brief Overview

Before further exploring the contemporary challenges affecting adolescent spirituality, it is important to explore the evolution of adolescent spirituality from its roots, to trace its trajectory and to have some sense of its course for the future. Although adolescent spirituality is a common phrase in pastoral ministry today, the emergence of the concept of adolescent spirituality is rather nuanced and novel within the historical context and understanding of the domain of spirituality. Although adolescent spirituality has evolved from various forms of catechetical practices, the Vatican II Council acted as the catalyst that created a real recognition for Catholics to address the needs surrounding adolescent spirituality.

Due to this evolution, some scholars date the advent of Catholic adolescent spirituality from the seventeenth and eighteenth centuries, based on the religious educational missions to outcasted and neglected adolescents, such as the work of John Baptist de le Salle and Elizabeth Ann Seton.[7] Other documents, from the Catholic Episcopate, state that Catholic adolescent spirituality emerged in congruence with Catholic youth ministry through the seminal document, A Vision of Youth Ministry, in 1976.[8] Nevertheless, the complexity of Catholic adolescent spirituality includes a catechetical component, as well as a formative awareness of social justice, liturgical understanding, deepening of prayer and relationship with God, peer collaboration, and a holistic development within the faith; in essence a mirror

5. McDonnell, "Interview with Thomas," 33.
6. Merton, "Learning to Live," 10.
7. Roberto, "History of Catholic Youth Ministry," 25–28.
8. Renewing the Vision, 19–20.

of the life of the apostles but offered through a lens deliberately meaningful for an adolescent.

The Foundations of Catholic Adolescent Spirituality

To trace the roots and development of a contemporary understanding of adolescent spirituality, it is important to explore the historical evolution of ministerial outreach to adolescents. For the sake of brevity, I have divided this history into four sections which will aid in the understanding of a holistic spirituality for adolescence beyond merely catechetical outreach:

1. The roots of adolescent spirituality: The 1800s
2. National recognition of adolescents and a social spirituality: The 1920s through the 1940s
3. A standardization toward holistic adolescent pastoral awareness: The 1960s to 1990s
4. Contemporary perspectives on adolescent spirituality: The 2000s to 2019

The following sections will briefly explore the themes of these four time periods as well as explore some features that helped form contemporary concepts of Catholic adolescent spirituality.

The Roots of Adolescent Spirituality: The 1800s

The roots of adolescent spirituality began to emerge beyond merely youth-aimed catechetical experiences with the creation of two youth-centered movements. These movements ultimately changed the face of the respect and recognition of dignity of adolescents in culture, namely: the creation of the Young Men's Christian Association (YMCA) as well as the work of John Bosco and his *Preventive System in the Education of the Young*.

The YMCA was originally founded in June 1844, by George Williams. Williams wanted to create an environment to help young men form habits for healthy Christian living, in contrast to the hedonistic lifestyles that he believed was a direct result of the urban sprawl during the Industrial Revolution in London. Williams also founded the YMCA based on the British Victorian belief of Muscular Christianity, a method of character-building popular at the time in British education. Muscular Christianity was a movement that argued faith development had an inherent connection with patriotic duty, discipline, self-sacrifice, manliness, and the moral and physical beauty of athleticism.[9] Muscular Christianity not only focused on education as an important component for adolescent development but also incorporated and recognized that an adolescent's physical development and engagement with sport, civic duty, and faith was essential for spiritual wholeness.

In the Catholic tradition, John Bosco, also felt a call to help adolescents affected by industrialization. He desired to offer homeless children and delinquent juveniles the opportunity to rise above a life of poverty or delinquency. Instead of merely offering such youth an education to better their job and life prospects, Bosco also challenged the prominent cultural view to recognize the dignity of the adolescents. Bosco's revolutionary vision in the *Preventive System in the Education of the Young*, from 1877, acknowledged that love is a more powerful force for change than punishment.[10] He argued that an authentic relationship with an adolescent based on charity would help form the relationship and bond needed for correction without resentment or desire for revenge. Bosco's insights offered a revolutionary step toward a greater awareness of the dignity of the adolescent as a human person, which is so often neglected when discussing a comprehensive approach to adolescent spirituality.

National Recognition of Adolescence and a Social Spiritualty: The 1920s through the 1940s

From the initial seeds of the 1800s further awareness of the need to distinguish the age of adolescence in society as well as the establishment of programs specifically geared for adolescents started to develop, these programs helped to showcase the talents and gifts that adolescents could contribute on a national scale, especially in America. Although one of the mentioned programs was in development well before the Great Depression, the three following organizations became nationally acknowledged

---

9. Although it could be claimed that the British-based Boy Scout & Girl Scout Movement, developed by Robert Baden-Powell and his sister Agnes Baden-Powell in 1912, ought to be included as a part of the evolution of adolescent spirituality I find that much of the Muscular Christianity underpinning that defined the YMCA parallels the foundations for the concept of Scouting.

10. Bosco, "Preventive System in the Education of the Young," §2.1.

during this period: Boys Town, the Catholic Youth Organization, and the National Youth Administration.

The 1920s and 1930s brought new challenges for American culture as a whole, through economic depression and a post-war listlessness. First established in 1917, the success of Boys Town came to the national consciousness in the 1930s. Father Edward Flanagan created an orphanage for at-risk children in Nebraska to engage youth in the maturation of self through civil duty. This dedicated focus later grew into a town, helping develop vocational skills for adulthood. The evolution of the work of Father Flanagan was later adapted into the Academy-Award-nominated film, *Boys Town* (1938) starring Spencer Tracey and Mickey Rooney. Father Flanagan's perspective of approaching adolescents acknowledged that youth did not have a future without being accepted fully in the present, which has become an essential aspect of ministry to youth today.[11]

Similar developments to help Catholic youth emerged in urban settings, in the 1930s, through the work of the Bishop of Chicago, Bernard Sheil, and the development of the Catholic Youth Organization (CYO). The CYO was established to help offer youth an opportunity for community activity apart from the temptation of criminality prevalent during the Prohibition Era. Although this was a Catholic response to the YMCA, the core components of the CYO also included the essential knowledge and active engagement of the social teachings of Catholic tradition. This social justice component led to a greater respect between adolescents and the local community.

On the national scene, President Roosevelt's New Deal also incorporated youth in the movement of societal hope. The National Youth Administration (NYA) focused on providing work and education for youth between the ages of sixteen and twenty-five. Although the NYA existed for a relatively short period of time, between 1935 and 1943, this governmental-sponsored program illustrated that youth can, and ought to, contribute to the social environment and develop a responsibility for civic and societal challenges, through work relief and employment efforts.

11. See Francis, "Christus Vivit," and Malewitz, "Who Am I? Why Am I Here?" 23–25.

A Standardization toward Holistic Adolescent Pastoral Awareness: The 1960s to 1990s

Although not all of these examples evolved from Catholic perspectives directly, one should not neglect the increased prominence of adolescents within the American cultural mindset. As American culture was cast into a social revolution during the late 1960s and early 1970s, the role of youth came to the forefront of the media and news. Hymns and anthems of change for a new perspective and youthful voice became the norm. Coincidentally, the Catholic Church reengaged the modern world with the message of Christ through the vision of the Vatican II Council. The combination of these events created the environment for an immediate and needed response of how the Church recognized the role of its youth.

Many groups of young people who had never possessed a voice began to be recognized and appreciated. It was during this time period that Eunice Kennedy Shiver, a Catholic social advocate, developed the Special Olympics for youth with disabilities for an unprecedented opportunity to participate in sports and competition.[12] This evolution of thought and social progress not only acknowledged the importance of the inclusion of adolescents of all disabilities but also offered a direct example of the power of sports in the life of youth, which will be discussed at length in chapter 8 of this manuscript.

In 1976, the United States Catholic Bishops officially released the seminal document, *A Vision of Youth Ministry*, which became the first comprehensive vision for a pastoral response to youth ministry in the Catholic Church. *A Vision of Youth Ministry* addressed youth ministry in a complete pastoral capacity by stating the need for holistic formation of body, mind, and spirit. Roughly a decade following this document, Pope John Paul II applied the Light-Life Movement, youth community-day concept which existed in Poland since the 1960s, into a world vision through the calling of the first World Youth Day. This movement, and international celebration, was not just for youth to engage the church but also became a witness that youth were a vibrant and active part of the whole church, as John Paul II stated:

> [Y]our youth is not just your own property, your personal property or the property of a generation: it belongs to the whole of that

---

12. The first Special Olympics was officially held in Chicago in 1968. Previously to 1968, the Shriver family opened their home as a summer camp, Camp Shriver, for youth with disabilities since 1963. See Mitchell, "Brave in the Attempt."

space that every man traverses in his life's journey, and at the same time it is a special possession belonging to everyone. It is a possession of humanity itself.[13]

World Youth Day has since grown into an international experience which continues to flourish and be a witness of the power and presence of the youth in the Church. In the late 1990s the United States Conference of Catholic Bishops (USCCB) reassessed the purpose and importance of youth ministry through *Renewing the Vision*. This comprehensive framework remains the standard of pastoral ministry for youth and a guide for pastoral and formational experiences for Catholic adolescents to mature physically, emotionally, intellectually, and spiritually.

Contemporary Perspectives on Adolescent Spirituality: The 2000s to 2019

The new millennium brought a new and energized focus on gathering information to understand and reengage the disconnectedness and dissatisfaction that seemed prominent between adolescents and the faith and rituals of the Christian experience. The National Study of Youth and Religion (NSYR) collected survey data on adolescent spirituality, ritual practices, and attitudes toward religious identity, perspectives, and engagement throughout America. Data from this comprehensive longitudinal study was collected through interviews with adolescents regarding their views, specifically on the role and importance that religion, ritual practices, and how personal beliefs effected their lives.

Significant trends and patterns of the responses from the NSYR have been examined by scholars over the recent decades. Kenda Creasy Dean, a professor at Princeton Theological Seminary and scholar of the NSYR data, offered that adolescent spirituality can be best described and characterized by the following three overarching themes: passion, advocacy, and authenticity.[14] Although these three aspects do not fully encompass the extent of adolescence, they nonetheless offer a frame of reference for dialogue about the psychological, spiritual, intellectual, and physical mindset and action of adolescents.

---

13. John Paul II, "Dilecti Amici," §1.

14. See Dean, *Almost Christian*, and Dean, *Practicing Passion*.

Following the footsteps of Dean's research, Catholic scholars also began to examine the NSYR data and its application to Catholic adolescent spirituality and youth ministry practices.[15] Since the NSYR, additional data on adolescent religious education, knowledge, moral, and ritual understanding has also been collected and analyzed through the National Catholic Educational Association.[16] Although this information has been available and taught to the scholarly minister communities, much of the wealth has not yet filtered into pastoral practice.

Most recently, though, two documents have readdressed the focus upon adolescent spirituality and youth ministry theory and practices for the twenty-first century on a broader scale: *The Joy of Adolescent Catechesis* and *Christus Vivit*, the youth-centered apostolic exhortation of Pope Francis. *The Joy of Adolescent Catechesis* was a document that acted as a concise synthesis for effective theory and practice of holistic ministry for adolescents, in light of the Pontiff's call of an evangelization of joy and desire for more integrative community.[17]

In 2019, Pope Francis pointedly challenged the church to the important role and contribution of youth through *Christus Vivit*. Pope Francis plainly stated: "We cannot just say that young people are the future of our world. They are its present; even now, they are helping to enrich it."[18] These words not only offer hope and insight into the call of adolescents within the voice of the church, but also call adolescents to journey in the world through a holistic vocation. This perspective of adolescents most closely resembles Thomas Merton's approach and parallels his relationships with adolescents captured throughout his correspondence, which will be illustrated throughout the following chapters.

Bridging the Gap: Through the Words and Experiences of Adolescents

Thomas Merton may seem like an odd exemplar to use when discussing adolescent spirituality; like most things over half-a-century ago, his influence

---

15. See Canales, *Noble Quest*; Mercadante, *Engaging a New Generation*; and Topping, *Case for Catholic Education*.

16. See Convey, *What Do Our Children Know About Their Faith?*, and Convey and Thompson, *Weaving Christ's Seamless Garment*.

17. Francis, "Evangelii Gaudium," §§112–19.

18. Francis, "Christus Vivit," §64.

may initially seem pretty much irrelevant to the contemporary issues, from an adolescent perspective. What insights could his life and writings offer in understanding adolescent spirituality in the digital age? The following chapters of this book will present themes through which Thomas Merton's life and writings parallel many themes and challenges of contemporary adolescence, through the lens of the themes of authenticity, passion, and advocacy.

As mentioned in the preface, collected student data will be woven into this text as evidence of the connection with the themes and writings of Thomas Merton. The following data illustrates the importance of the desire of self-discovery for authenticity, passion, and advocacy within the words and thoughts of the adolescent students. The student journals collected over the course of the study offered the bulk of the data that explored self-discovery for authenticity and advocacy. The following data offer some initial examples from the student responses;[19] these comments were based on a reflective activity about on a social outreach documentary film, *The Human Experience*, shown to the students during the explorative curriculum.[20]

> Matthew: It was empowering to me. These 2 brothers really went for it. I want to go for it like that and make a major change in the process. Through my going for it, I want to make a difference in our world.[21]

> Robert: I really liked watching the film. It opened a window to something I have never experienced [*sic*]. I have never seen so much poverty, but out of that poverty was happiness . . . This made me question my own happiness because I have so much but I am not as happy.[22]

> James: I want to do something to make people know who I am. I want to do it in a good way though . . . I want to make the world a better place.[23]

Passion was also displayed by many students throughout the course of their dialogues, but most clearly in the group activities such as the Jenga game and the drum circle used in the exploratory curriculum. As the

19. All names used throughout this manuscript referring to student data and quotations are pseudonyms to ensure the confidentiality of the participants of the original study.

20. See: Kinnane, *The Human Experience*.

21. Collected artifacts: personal journal, April 20, 2018.

22. Collected artifacts: personal journal, April 20, 2018.

23. Collected artifacts: personal journal, April 20, 2018.

following vignettes indicate, students encouraged, celebrated, mourned, and collaborated together to try to keep their towers up as long as possible. While the response of the drum circle activity were similar to the dynamics of a sports team, where the students relied on their teammates to succeed, and they then celebrated their experience together.

> Harold [verbal response: excitedly, eager to share]: well, we decided that we were going to follow a system so we wouldn't bicker. We had a talking stick, and the one who holds it is the one who talks. So, we passed it around and that's how we communicated so that we wouldn't talk over each other . . . yea, its's right here, gimme a sec [rummages through his materials and brings out a pencil that has a small feather taped to the eraser end; proudly displays the stick for the class].[24]

> Timothy [written response]: The circle reminded me that this school, the church, and many teams are like that small drum circle. It takes many people to create something great. It also reminded me that I am a part of something greater than myself. Not just the drum circle, but many other things I do are a part of something greater than myself.[25]

The data collected from these experiences indicate that the students' interpretation of the topics related to the lived-experience of adolescents and directly connected to the aspects of self-discovery, passion, and advocacy that define adolescent spirituality.

24. Large group discussion, April 24, 2018.
25. Collected artifacts: worksheet, May 1, 2018.

2

Thomas Merton

A Life of Authenticity, Passion, and Advocacy

During the first period, after entering the monastery, I was totally isolated from all outside influences and was working with what I accumulated before entering . . . Most people judge me entirely by this period, either favorably or unfavorably, and do not realize that I have changed a great deal. The second period was a time when I began to open up again to the world, began reading psychoanalysis, Zen Buddhism, existentialism and other things like that . . . It appears that I am now evolving further, with studies on Zen and a new kind of experiential creative drive in prose poetry, satire, etc.[1]

IN THE SUMMER OF 1968, responding to an inquiry about dividing the significant periods of his writings, Thomas Merton offered one of the final recorded reflections of the evolution of his authorship. As demonstrated above, Merton had a clear recognition that his interests had evolved considerably since he first entered monastic life. Looking back on the breadth of his writings today, it can be a complicated and almost insurmountable task to frame, with clarity, a complete perspective of his complex and ever-developing view of the world. This manuscript will only attempt to examine one vein of the myriad topics of Merton's writings.

1. Merton, "Letter to Sr. J. M., June 17, 1968," 11.

Since there already exist many texts on the life and experiences of Thomas Merton, I will not offer an extensive biography here. My hope for this brief section of biographical information is to include insights for the reader into the context of Thomas Merton's life and writings which primarily relate to the topic of adolescent spirituality. Although the following introduction may not satisfy Merton scholars, or those quite unfamiliar with Merton, my desire is to offer insights of his life to explore those moments that significantly bear meaning for the topic at hand. This chapter will briefly explore the experiences that developed his desire of a life full of authenticity, passion, and advocacy that can relate to adolescence.

Merton: Born for Authenticity

Thomas Merton was born on January 31, 1915, in Prades, France. His parents, Owen Merton and Ruth Jenkins, labored as artists and traveled throughout Europe during his early life. As the dangers of World War I escalated, the Merton family moved to America finding security with Ruth's parents. As they lived in America, the Merton family welcomed a second boy, John Paul, in 1918.

Before the family could relocate to Europe Ruth developed stomach cancer and succumbed to the disease in 1921, when Thomas was six years old. After the death of his wife, Owen Merton resumed his livelihood painting and traveling to the Bahamas and Europe. Thomas Merton accompanied his father throughout most of these travels, while his younger brother, John Paul, stayed in America with his grandparents. During most of his father's European travels, young Thomas was often left at boarding schools throughout France and England. During this time, Thomas Merton recalled being a victim to the isolating effects of verbal and physical bullying, which will be explored in chapter 12 of this manuscript.

Merton: A Passionate Adolescent and Young Adult

Thomas Merton's life was affected once again by tragedy during his adolescence. In 1931, Merton was informed that his father was diagnosed with cancer. After the death of his father, later that year, Merton was left an orphan in England while still in secondary schooling. He completed his education in England, living on a pension and virtually unsupervised. Thomas

Merton recalled that the death of his father saddened and depressed him, and that he felt a great void and hopelessness at the time.[2]

Thomas finished his secondary education, visited his remaining family in America, and traveled throughout Europe during the summer before entering his post-secondary studies. This period of Merton's life could be best classified similar to contemporary stereotypical lifestyles of students in first-year college without supervision, one of excess. Merton honestly stated that he was excessive with drinking and carousing during this period of his life.[3]

Merton persisted in a strong individualistic perspective in relation to the world during his young adult life, captured in the passion and recklessness of independent youth. In the fall of 1933, he entered Clare College, Cambridge on scholarship. During this period Merton's behavior was reckless. Scholars have mentioned that, although he certainly fathered a child, Merton lost his scholarship to Clare College due to poor attentiveness and grades.[4] He was eventually forced to move to America, closer to his grandparents and brother because of his instable living.

In America, Merton enrolled at Columbia University and his restless nature began to settle through the influence of a new community of friends and engaging instructors. Mark Van Doren and Dan Walsh, two professors at Columbia, had lasting impressions upon him. The relationships with Van Doren and Walsh evolved from mere instructors into lifelong friendships.

Merton: The Contemplative

After Merton concluded his master's degree, he felt a calling to discern the vocation of a Catholic religious. He was initially encouraged by Dan Walsh, his teacher, friend, and mentor, to inquire about joining the Franciscan friars.[5] After the disappointment of a rejection from the Franciscan community Merton spent a year teaching English at St. Bonaventure College, New York, in 1941. It was during this year that he took an Easter retreat to the Abbey of Our Lady of Gethsemani, near Bardstown, Kentucky. He felt immediately drawn to the simplistic and rustic life of the Cistercians. He

2. Merton, *Seven Storey Mountain*, 94.

3. Merton, *Seven Storey Mountain*, 137, 173–74, 181–82. See also Horan, *Franciscan Heart of Thomas Merton*, 40–41.

4. Merton, *Seven Storey Mountain*, 138–41. Also see Forest, *Living with Wisdom*, 35–36.

5. Horan, *Franciscan Heart of Thomas Merton*, 59–72.

was so moved from the retreat experience that he inquired about a monastic vocation with the Cistercians, and entered as a postulant with the monastery in December 1941. After entering the community and signaling a change of character and his dedication to a new way of life, Merton was given a habit, a set of clothes identifying his new life in the community, and given the monastic name, Louis.[6]

With the Cistercian Order, Father Louis's writing talents were acknowledged, recognized, and encouraged by his superior, Dom Fox. Merton was called upon to write for the community, and with the permission of the abbot, the head of the order, he was encouraged to write his own reflections of his call to the monastic life. In 1946, Merton submitted his spiritual autobiography *The Seven Storey Mountain* for publication. *The Seven Storey Mountain* was published in 1948, and became a national bestseller the following year. From 1949 to his death in 1968, Merton was challenged to find balance between his identity as a celebrity author and his monastic life.

Because of the attention of his writings and the subsequent influx of vocations to the Cistercians, Merton was called upon by his superior to serve as master of scholastics and lead the formation of the students studying for

6. Merton, *Seven Storey Mountain*, 422.

priesthood. Later he was called to serve as novice master, overseeing the formation of men just entering monastic life.[7] These roles brought Merton directly into the role of spiritual guide and teacher for men throughout their discernment and into their first years in communal life with the Trappist community. Over four hundred hours of audio recordings of Merton's sermons, talks, and conferences are archived at the Thomas Merton Center on the campus of Bellarmine University in Louisville, Kentucky. With his additional time, Merton wrote poetry, spiritual books, short reflections, and commentaries on numerous cultural challenges within society, as well as sustained numerous correspondences.

Merton: The Advocate

Thomas Merton's views, embodied within his writings and life, evolved substantially as he matured. As Merton came to deeper awareness of his vocation and evolved in his relationship with God, his behavior likewise evolved into a more compassionate, understanding, and unitive force with all aspects of humanity. To appreciate the whole corpus of Merton's writings, it is important to look at the passion of his reckless youthfulness as well as the mystical wisdom he demonstrated throughout his monastic life, as it all exemplified his voice for authentic hope and change, and offered a parallel of the potential expected hope and maturity of adolescence.

Like his friend Dorothy Day, the American social activist and co-founder of the *Catholic Worker*, Thomas Merton referred to himself as a *Catholic anarchist.*[8] He felt a call and had a passion for advocacy and social change beyond the common Catholic standards of his time. Throughout the 1950s and 1960s, Merton's writings highlighted the dignity of the human person, supported nonviolence and the Civil Rights Movement, and acknowledged the inherent unity of all humanity through ecumenism and interreligious dialogue well before the official proclamations of Vatican II. Although he had an interest in Eastern spirituality in his college years, Merton's interest in Eastern religions and ecumenism bloomed again later in his life.

---

7. Thomas Merton served the Abbey of Gethsemani as master of scholastics from 1951–55, and master of novices from 1955–65.

8. Labrie, *Thomas Merton and the Inclusive Imagination*, 207.

In 1968, Merton was able to experience pilgrimage to Alaska, California, and the East to tangibly engage topics and places he only previously studied from afar. With the permission of his abbot, he was able to attend and give a keynote address for the Aide à l'Implantation Monastique Conference on monastic renewal, in Bangkok, Thailand. Throughout his journey, he was able to spend time talking with prominent religious leaders from the Eastern traditions, including the Dalai Lama. On December 10, 1968, after giving a lecture entitled "Marxism and Monastic Perspectives," Merton died from accidental electrocution during an afternoon shower. The official Thai death certificate stated that the cause of death was due to cardiac failure and accidental electrocution.[9]

Merton: Correspondence with Adolescents

Although Thomas Merton had limited exposure to adolescents throughout his adult life, his approach to self-discovery and desire for a holistic unity in the individual and community can continue to speak to the challenges of contemporary adolescents. A collection of Merton's correspondence

9. Weakland, *Pilgrim in a Pilgrim Church*, 166.

with young people was originally complied by preeminent Merton scholar Robert Daggy, who also wrote a brief reflection about Merton's relationship with young people.[10] This text seeks to continue and expand the exploration of Daggy's initial reflection of Merton's relationship with adolescents, and how themes from his writing could help with addressing challenges with adolescent spirituality today.

It is important to note that the following list of Merton's communication and experience with adolescents was compiled here to explore themes discussed within those letters and offer further insights for ministry of contemporary adolescents. The list below only includes formally documented correspondence between Thomas Merton and junior high or high school aged students (namely sixth to twelfth grade), or adolescents who directly impacted the life and writing of Merton.[11] The following list will be presented chronologically in relation to the life of Merton.

For reader clarity, Thomas Merton's longest and most preserved example of a relationship with an adolescent was with Suzanne Butorovich. There were over a dozen letters shared between June 1967 and Merton's Asian trip in 1968. It is well-documented that Merton met and had dinner with Suzanne and her family while he was in California in 1968, before his trip to the East. Suzanne was also the youngest and furthest traveled visitor to attend Merton's funeral at Gethsemani.[12] The conversation within these letters illustrate a relationship that evolved from an initial acquaintance correspondence to an authentic friendship which ultimately became a familial charity. Merton mentioned Suzanne to the monks at the monastery and also included mention of her in his other correspondences.[13]

10. Merton, *Road to Joy*, 308–69; and Daggy, "Road to Joy: Thomas Merton's Letters to and About Young People," 52–71.

11. There are more letters that Merton received and replied with young people, such as college-aged, family friends, or from anonymous or untraceable individuals, which have not been included here for the sake of clarity.

12. See Morgan Atkinson's documentary film, *Many Stories and Last Days of Thomas Merton*.

13. Two examples of Merton's inclusion of correspondence of Suzanne to his adult correspondences are found in *The Hidden Ground of Love*; such as a July 22, 1967 letter to June J. Yungblut (p. 636), and an August 11, 1967 letter to W. H. Ferry (p. 232).

Annotated Collection of Thomas Merton and Adolescents

1. Sr. Marialein Lorenz's high school students (April to June 1949—Mobile, Alabama) and Gloria Sylvester Bennett (August 1966; January 1967—Chicago, Illinois):

    1949—Theme—Authenticity: Gratitude; Spiritual reality over materialism

    1966; 1967—Theme—Advocacy: Racism

    Sr. Lorenz, a teacher at Heart of Mary, an all-black high school in Mobile, Alabama, had her students write letters to Merton in 1949; they also sent him the gift of an amice, which he wore during his first mass, as well as an ordination present.[14] Merton's response, besides acting as a letter of gratitude for the gracious gifts, also reminded the students about the need to search for God's goal throughout their lives: happiness. This theme becomes the crux of Merton's later manuscript, *No Man Is an Island*, published six years later.

    Throughout this correspondence, Merton pointedly stated that the adolescents need to search beyond the lure of materialism for the truths of a spiritual reality. He encouraged them to follow the Holy Ghost and to follow the good example of the Catholic education that they received. His letter also explored the hope and power of the Blessed Lady in America and bringing hope to those in hopeless poverty within communist China.

    A testament to the power of this letter was that one of the students from Sr. Lorenz's class, Gloria, wrote to Merton roughly a decade-and-a-half later, during the height of the Civil Rights Movement. The connection and hope offered through Merton's letter to an adolescent community later came to fruition and inspired an adult to seek wisdom and guidance through trust and sincerity. In the first letter, Merton acknowledged the gift Gloria sent: a copy of her husband's 1965 book *Black and White*, which examined race relations in the United States at the time. Merton was thrilled with the gift as he acknowledged that he was always in need of accurate information about the state of the country outside of the walls of the monastery.

    The second letter from Gloria was specifically geared toward the experiences of racism that her children received in Chicago schools, especially at the hands of their professed religious teachers, the nuns.

14. Merton, *Road to Joy*, 314–17.

In his response, Merton discussed the dignity of the human person as well as weaknesses of the human person.

2. Susan Neer (December 1963—Saint Ann, Missouri)
    Theme—Advocacy: Racism, Responding to hatred
    The conversation between Merton and Susan Neer focused on the question racism in America. Merton's response to the adolescent's query authentically addressed the problems of real attitudes of racism, while exploring the psychological nature of humanity. Although people could be inherently nice, there are parts of the country where racism exists in a tangible and horrific way. The concluding thoughts posed by Merton acknowledged that violence will not end hatred, and left the response to such hatred in the culture open and in the hands of the adolescent to challenge, engage, and change her future's culture.

3. Jim Frost (January 1964—Waterloo, Iowa)
    Theme—Advocacy and Passion: The inherent goodness of life and nature
    Although Jim Frost's letter to Merton was an "ask the author" assignment for school, it simply just asked him for a response, without expectation. Merton was amused by its brevity and offered the adolescent insights on the need to appreciate the goodness of life and nature. Through small anecdotes, Merton encouraged a service-mindedness toward the land and humanity's call to be stewards of it.

4. Denise McNair and the 16th Street Baptist Church Bombing (October 1964—Birmingham, Alabama)
    Theme—Advocacy: Racism, Terror, Trauma, Grief
    On September 15, 1963, a bombing occurred at the 16th Street Baptist Church in Birmingham, Alabama. While more than twenty individuals were injured, four young girls between the ages of eleven and fourteen years old were killed. *LOOK* magazine published an article which had photos of the children who were murdered during the explosion. In that article the pictures of Carole Denise McNair, one of the victims, included common and ordinary activities of a young girl (such as holding a doll, dressing up, and waving to a camera), but all of the pictures had a haunting and ephemeral beauty, noting the loss and trauma of the horrific situation.[15]

---

15. Huie, "Death of an Innocent," 23–25.

Thomas Merton was so haunted by one of the photos that he was moved to keep the clipping from that magazine article, in his journal— as a constant reminder of someone who never learned how to hate.[16] Merton was also moved, by the horrific attack, to write a letter to the McNair family as well as two poems inspired by the event entitled: "And the Children of Birmingham" as well as "Picture of a Black Child with a White Doll."[17] Although Merton prominently wrote about the importance of the recognition of human dignity since his mystical experience documented in *Conjectures of a Guilty Bystander*,[18] the lion's share of his writings on nonviolence, the call for a zealous renewal of the dignity of the human person, and the need for communal human unity came after the experience of the death of these girls.

5. Antoinette M. Costa (May 1965—Taunton, Massachusetts)
  Theme—Authenticity: Responding to public opinion; Staying true to one's self

  Antoinette Costa's letter requested help regarding a class research paper. In this correspondence Merton responded by reflecting on his thoughts and experience of critics about his writings as well as topics that he was in the process of writing. His advice for Costa, as an aspiring writer, focused on not allowing critical comments to bother her as an author—as they may just be responding to a piece of work or art through a particular ideological lens. Merton encouraged that a particular critique does not mean that the critic knows anything about the authentic person behind the art or authorship.

6. Geraldine McNamara (November 1965—unknown location)
  Theme—Authenticity: Vocation; Trappist life; Dialogue

  Geraldine's letter was seeking information about the life of a Trappist through a series of predefined questions. It is recorded that Geraldine read Merton's letter to her class and then replied to Merton with their reaction.

  Merton briefly responded to each question outlining the day of a Trappist. He discussed the eating habits at the monastery, explained the vows, silence and the sign language used to communicate on the

16. Merton, *Road to Joy*, 332–33.

17. See Merton, *Collected Poems of Thomas Merton*, 335–37, 626–27. The poem "Picture of a Black Child with a White Doll" is included and further explored in chapter 10.

18. See the 4th and Walnut experience, as described by Merton in *Conjectures of a Guilty Bystander*, 153–56.

grounds. He concluded the letter by encouraging her to live a life of balance and discernment in the midst of the cultural extremes of the 1960s.

7. Jan Boggs (February 1966—Niskayuna, New York)
    Theme—Passion: Art and Poetry; Peer respect (between an adult and adolescent)
    Merton's correspondence with Jan Boggs revolved around a query for a definition of a poem for a class assignment. Merton's definition of a poem was to the point but expansive, exploring the deep and challenging nature of symbolism in poetry. It is recorded that Jan replied thanking Merton for his letter, and stated: "in a world where so many adults have a low opinion of teenagers in general, it means a lot to us when adults treat us like young adults."[19]

8. Tony Boyd (March 1967—Ashland, Kentucky)
    Theme—Passion: Music
    Tony was a junior high student who wrote Merton seeking information about Kentucky for a class scrapbook project. In his response, Merton amusingly stated: "you are the first person who ever picked me out as an authority on music."[20] Throughout this letter, Merton discussed his musical skill on the bongos,[21] as well as his enjoyment of the music of Johnny Cash and Gregorian Chant. He then offered very basic information about Kentucky, which primarily revolved around the history and work of the monastery.

9. Susan Chapulis (April 1967—Waterbury, Connecticut)
    Theme—Authenticity: Monastic life; Goodness of creation; Silence
    Susan Chapulis was a junior high student who wrote to Merton seeking information about monks and monastic life. Merton's response is a well-worded response for a junior high student; it was concise and at a level that could be easily understood by a young adolescent. He discussed the life of silence, retreat from the world, and connection with nature. In a moment of humor Merton stated: "A monk who lives all by himself in the woods is called a hermit. There is a Rock 'n Roll outfit called Herman and his Hermits [sic] but they

---

19. Merton, "Letter to Jan Boggs, February 9 1966," 338.

20. Merton, "Letter to Tony Boyd, March 20 1967," 346–47.

21. Merton's musical skill, although not examined frequently, is still well-remembered and discussed by individuals like Richard Sisto. Two photographs of Ralph Eugene Meatyard that captured Merton playing bongos immortalized this talent. See Meatyard, *Father Louie: Photographs of Thomas Merton*, 101–2.

are not the same thing."[22] Merton concluded by encouraging Susan to remember God's desire for human happiness and to search for that happiness throughout her life.

10. Besti Baeten (October 1967—West De Pere, Wisconsin)
   Theme—Advocacy: Racism and Civil Rights

Betsi Baeten was a junior high student who wrote to Merton asking for a few insights about the Civil Rights Movement, as the students in her class were planning to present a panel at an upcoming PTA meeting for their parents. She specifically asked Merton to write in language that a teenager could understand and convey. Merton's response specifically explored, through a psychological insight, why people label and separate others by labels. He explained that the authentic gospel message is to love but our culture has not learned how to do that. Pertinent sections of this letter will appear in chapter 12 of this manuscript, and lays the foundations of understanding unity versus isolation in community identity.

11. Suzanne Butorovich (June 1967 to Fall 1968—Campbell, California)
   Theme—Advocacy, Authenticity, and Passion: Popular culture; True friendship

Suzanne Butorovich was a sixteen-year-old high school student from California who initially solicited Merton for a contribution to her underground student paper, the *Clique Courier*. Suzanne's initial invitation, unassuming and innocent, set into motion the longest recorded relationship that Thomas Merton had with an adolescent.[23] In an interview regarding the correspondence and friendship, Suzanne mentioned that she never expected a reply, nor did she fully know Merton's reputation as an author when she sent the letter.[24]

The Merton Center has cataloged twenty-three letters written by Merton to Suzanne. Throughout their correspondence, Merton exemplified compassion and respect toward Suzanne's questions and

22. Merton, "Letter to Susan Chapulis, April 10, 1967," 351.

23. Although most of Merton's letters with Suzanne have been published in *The Road to Joy*, there remains sections of unpublished letters and postcards in the Thomas Merton Center at Bellarmine University that shed further insight into how Thomas Merton approached and respected Suzanne, as an adolescent and as a peer.

24. Morgan Atkinson's documentary film, *The Many Stories and Last Days of Thomas Merton*, includes in-depth interviews with individuals close to Merton during the last year of his life, including Suzanne Butorovich Demattei.

answered her as an interested friend, at times including teasing, humor, and jest. Merton's responses through the letters indicated that he not only regarded her as an equal in spirit, but family: he shared his poetry, early copies of writings, and asked for her feedback on his work.

Likewise, the people and events important to her, such as the death of the Beatles' manager Brian Epstein, lyrics of Bob Dylan, and music of Jefferson Airplane, were treated with sincerity and respect by Merton. He offered his insight and spiritual perspectives on topics about authors like J. R. R. Tolkien, O. Henry, and Kahlil Gibran; Zen Buddhism; music from India; and cooking Kasha.[25] The mutuality illustrated through the communications of this relationship offer insights of a deeper awareness and appreciation of the spirituality that is present in the lives of adolescents which Merton directly recognized and appreciated.

12. Philip J. Cascia (April 1968—Bloomfield, Connecticut)
    Theme—Advocacy and Authenticity: Ecumenism; Social Change
    Philip Cascia was an adolescent who wrote to Merton for his insights about a term paper on ecumenism, as well as many of the changes of liturgy that affected the church after Vatican II. Merton addressed topics on the benefit of ecumenism, the importance of lay ministers in the church, his thoughts on celibacy, and the role of good music in liturgy: folk and Gregorian. Merton clearly stated that real and beneficial social change should be purposeful and have an essential meaning, and not to change just for the sake of change.

The following chapters will illustrate that Thomas Merton was keenly aware of the concerns and challenges of adolescents and was touched by the lives of young people who affected, changed, and evolved his life and perspectives of the dignity of the human person. Merton did not treat adolescents as having less value than adults or having less value than himself, but treated each encounter with an adolescent as a respected peer. Merton's communication with adolescents had an awareness of peer respect, a genuine interest in the other, and a willingness of honest vulnerability on intellectual and mature subjects that challenged the whole growth of the individual, navigating maturity from youth to young adulthood, through authenticity, passion, and advocacy.

---

25. Merton, *Road to Joy*, 308–12.

3

Education

The Roots of Self-Discovery

I believe education means more than just imparting "knowledge." It means the formation of the whole person.[1]

It might seem like the topic of education is an odd place to begin a discussion about adolescent spirituality, but education stands at the very foundation of a whole formation of the body, mind, and spirit, toward authentic self-discovery. As mentioned previously, the roots of Catholic adolescent spirituality evolved from various forms of educational theory and practices. Today, though, adolescents often dismiss the importance of education, stating that the process is boring or is just about receiving a grade, but the reality of the role of education in each of our lives is part of a much more profound journey.

Although the quotation at the beginning of this chapter is brief, I would argue that it stands as one of the most foundational aspects of Merton's thought throughout this manuscript, and a fitting beginning to explore a holistic approach to addressing adolescent spirituality. For Merton, whose life became a vocation that revolved around the formation of others, this statement stands as the bedrock, or creed, for all other human interaction. Merton stated that knowledge alone is not the end goal, but

1. Merton, "Letter to Mary Declan Martin, April 1, 1968," 364.

is only part of the educational process. His insight of education as being the journey that forms the whole person, carries a gravity to the reality that authentic education does not end through a graduation ceremony, or conferral of a degree, but is a lifelong exploration scaffolded by reflections and experiences that continually define an individual's character, action, and meaning in life. The awareness of the journey toward wholeness was not innate in the adolescent Merton, though; it was experienced and later embodied from the witnesses of mentors and friends he viewed as great and revered educators.

The State of Education: Perspectives on Learning and Living

Education is seen as the backbone of our culture. It is so valued that it is consistently debated in elections and local school districts, though there has yet been consensus regarding the best educational practices or ways to fund educational systems. The teachers' strike in Los Angeles, at the beginning of 2019, offered a creditable and sobering witness to the need for further discussion and exploration for a financial reform in the educational structure across the nation.[2] Questions regarding educational funding, the worth and value of educational policy, school vouchers, increased tuition, and the reassessment of educational expenses based on cost analysis seem to suppose the perspective that the contemporary state of education is viewed more often in terms of business commodities rather than a process of holistic human development. If the educational system, composed of its complex administrative structures and political lobbying, is merely another business entity in the American culture, what would an honest evaluation and assessment of the success of its production reveal?

The current model of educational standards evolved from societal needs established during the industrial revolution. Standardized and mandatory educational policies were originally structured from a top-down, reductionistic society of the early twentieth century. As mentioned previously, the industrial revolution influenced new perspectives on views of adolescent formation that affected various dimensions of society. Based on the needs and productivity of an industrial society educational psychologists like Edward Thorndike and curriculum theorists like John Franklin Bobbitt championed a utilitarian vision for curriculum and education

2. Medina et al., "Los Angeles Teachers Strike, Disrupting Classes for 500,000 Students."

standards. They argued that this perspective could ensure the continued growth of the economic boom of the American landscape.[3] Within their vision, education was approached as an avenue for development to become a productive unit for society where the industrial productivity of the society would become the ultimate unit of measure to determine the success of the educational system. During the same generation, John Dewey, the educational philosopher and psychologist, argued that students should be educated to be productive units within society but also be taught to develop a democratic moral perspective, an essential component within the curriculum standards to continue the values and success of the American ethos.[4]

Thorndike, Bobbitt, and Dewey all contributed aspects of the educational vision and curriculum perspectives that were a fitting foundation for the American twentieth century which were grounded upon industry, nationalism, and systematic productivity. Each student-citizen was envisioned to play an important part within the melting pot of America; a role their style of education prepared, produced, and sustained.[5] Along with the industrial perspective of education, measurements to assess the effectiveness of such a structure were quantitatively essential and rather easy to calculate: a numerical value would be attributed to measure the proficiency of skills predetermined for success as an adult citizen. The worth and value of the production of the educational system would then be evaluated on how well it produced capable and prepared students as adults to promote the goods and needs of the society.

Such preestablished quantitative standards continue to exist embedded in the consciousness of the educational structure, such as in the forms of assessments that measure knowledge through reductionistic answers, usually predefined and with limited availability for personal creative expression and exploration. But contemporary student-learners face a new challenge as well as a new American landscape, such as the decline of nationalism, the increase of crosscultural appreciation and an expanding global job market, instant communication, and a deeper reverence of collaboration.[6] In contrast to the goals of the twentieth century, contemporary pedagogical needs a

3. Bobbitt, "Actual Objectives of the Present-Day High School," 450–467, and Pinar et al., *Understanding Curriculum*.

4. See curriculum theorists such as Henderson and Kesson, *Curriculum Wisdom*.

5. Jackson, "Shifting Visions of the Curriculum," 118–33.

6. See Fullan, *New Meaning of Educational Change*, as well as Malewitz and Pacheco, "No Soy de Aquí ni Soy de Allá."

more global and unitive philosophical contrast to the educational goals of an individual, industrial American educational structure.[7]

The State of Education: Perspectives for Self-Discovery

In contrast to the nationalism of Dewey, and the productive expectations of Thorndike, European educators like Maria Montessori and Luigi Giussani offered pedagogical perspectives focused on the quality of instruction for student learner-based education.[8] These perspectives were not completely foreign in the American consciousness, though it was less popular and often approached as suspect. At the collegiate level, the view of education as a student-centered process of self-discovery could be exemplified in the pedagogical perspectives of the Columbia University professor of literature Mark Van Doren, and the Stanford professor of art and education Elliot Eisner; while in distinctly religious educational perspectives exemplars such as Thomas Merton and Parker Palmer offer insights into the necessity of a holistic awareness of relationships and the human person for authentic educational praxis.[9] As Merton stated: "The way to find the real 'world' is not merely to measure and observe what is outside us, but to discover our own inner ground. For that is where the world is, *first* of all: in my deepest self."[10] Such human-centered perspectives from educators offer examples of a reengaging of education as a relational process based on qualitative inquiry, in contrast to a pure numerical quantitative assessment; where the unique gifts and talents of students can have the opportunity to develop and become expansive instead of constrictive.

To develop universal skills to approach an unknown future and prepare for the unexpected demands within such realities, it is important

7. See Abeles and Congdon's documentary *Race to Nowhere*, which explores contemporary challenges of adolescents, parents, and teachers as well as the changing dynamic of the pressures of a standardized educational system; and Abeles and Rubenstein, *Beyond Measure*.

8. Montessori, "General Notes on the Education of the Senses," 223–29; also Giussani, *Risk of Education*.

9. Del Prete, "Thomas Merton on Mark Van Doren," 16–18; Eisner, "Educating the Whole Person," 37–41; and Eisner, "Questionable Assumptions about Schooling," 648–57; also see Merton, "Learning to Live," 3–24; Palmer, *Courage to Teach*; and Block, *Classroom*.

10. Merton, "Contemplation in a World of Action," 154.

to reflect on the very core and nature of education, especially for adolescents.[11] The challenges facing contemporary adolescents are not limited to geographical boundaries, as in previous generations. Access to the internet now offers more information and access to knowledge than previous generations could have imagined. But there is a difference between information and knowledge, and a considerable difference between knowledge and wisdom. Here Merton's insights, from the quotation at the beginning of this chapter, resound even more clearly. Contemporary education practices for adolescents must acknowledge and discuss the nature of the student, based on the recognition of balance: between the student-discoverer and the student-citizen.

Education for Adolescents:
Inquiry and Theological Reflection

Today, more than ever, there is a desire to search for human authenticity, a call to acknowledge and respect diversity, as well as a call of an honest assessment of educators and the abilities and the potentiality of students. This human authenticity does not just drive motivations, behaviors, and production, but it also drives financial contributions and the desire of how such contributions are distributed and what materials become a mandatory part of the educational process, such as technologies. Pope Francis stated that formation of the whole person is an essential part of education for contemporary times to face the challenges of an information-saturated society: "We are living in an information-driven society which bombards us indiscriminately with data—all treated as being of equal importance—and which leads to remarkable superficiality in the area of moral discernment."[12] It is not the amount of information that a student receives which defines their education, but rather how and why the student uses the information in their formation and maturation of whom they become.

Lifelong educator and Merton scholar Thomas Del Prete explored the essential nature of the education of the whole person through the writings and examples of Thomas Merton. Though there exists very little direct connection between Merton and a concrete pedagogical vision, Del Prete was able to distill Merton's educational convictions through trends found through his texts and conference lectures.

11. Eisner, "Preparing for Today and Tomorrow." 6–10.
12. Francis, "Evangelii Gaudium," §64.

One's essential freedom is not realized in imitation of social status or standard or in accordance with any other externally imposed measure. Merton's message is clear: An education which would safeguard the personal capacity for free, creative, and genuine relationship with others in the world must ultimately provide for self-discovery.[13]

Other contemporary Catholic educational theorists have begun to advocate this essential approach to education. Education is the process from which an individual learns and matures throughout life. Educational philosopher and theology professor Ryan N. S. Topping stated: "Education is not a thing. It is a method."[14] Education understood as a method should be experienced as a process to shape and form a human being as a whole person. Through youth and young adulthood, effective instruction becomes the touchstone that a student uses to acquire and develop the needed skills that lay a foundation for adulthood.

Merton: Life, as a Journey of Experiences

Thomas Merton is not primarily remembered as an educator. Throughout his life though, Merton had multiple experiences, as well as monastic occupations, that could directly fall under a natural pedagogical label. One could also argue that his numerous writings and correspondence evolved into an indirect teacher/mentor relationship with many readers and followers of his writings. Some of the traditional instructional experiences of Thomas Merton would be his teaching a semester extension course in English composition at Columbia University in fall 1939, and English courses at St. Bonaventure's College, from the fall semester of 1940 to December 1941. After entering the monastery, Merton also held the educational roles of master of scholastics, from 1951–55, where he was in charge of the formation of the students studying to become priests, as well as master of novices, from 1955–65, where he was in charge of the formation of men entering monastic life.

13. Del Prete, *Thomas Merton and the Education of the Whole Person*, 31.

14. Topping, *Renewing the Mind*, 8.

Education was in his blood. In a letter to a college student, Mary Declan Martin, Merton acknowledged that his grandmother was a teacher in New Zealand.[15] In the same letter, he recounted and briefly discussed his own experiences as a formal educator at Bonaventure, but firmly stated that he believed that his work as novice master within Gethsemani was a duty within the concept of education. Thomas Merton's perspective on education nonetheless played an integral part of his vocation as a writer, as well as throughout his personal relationships with those around him. He did not confine education to a constrained program or a limited series of topics for mastery, Merton clearly believed that the totality of the experiences throughout an individual's life is education, namely the formation of the whole person.

Throughout *The Seven Storey Mountain*, as well as in his article "On Remembering Monsieur Delmas,"[16] Thomas Merton takes great time,

15. Merton, "Letter to Mary Declan Martin, April 1, 1968," 364.

16. Monsieur Delmas was a French teacher that Merton had during his childhood. Although Merton had little acknowledgement toward the French education he received in *The Seven Storey Mountain*, he later revisited experiences with Monsieur Delmas with more fondness in a reflection on education later in his life. See Merton, "On Remembering Monsieur Delmas"; Del Prete, *Thomas Merton and the Education of the Whole Person*, 148, 153–54; and Forest, *Living with Wisdom*, 15.

consideration, and reflection into aspects that he believed defined engaging educational experiences and exemplified excellent teaching techniques. While at Columbia University, Merton stated his impression of two particularly exceptional and life-altering professors, Mark Van Doren and Dan Walsh. He argued that both educators illustrated a simple, direct, and authentic approach to education. While reflecting on the pedagogical importance of the life of Merton, Thomas Del Prete explained that Merton was captivated with Van Doren's honesty and search for truth.[17] Walsh, while not only a teacher, became a trusted educator, guide, and confidant of Merton's Christian awakening and discernment, and lifelong friend.[18] From these experiences Merton's own perspective of education evolved into what he defined as the process to show a person "how to define himself authentically and spontaneously in relation to his world—not to impose a prefabricated definition of the world, still less an arbitrary definition of the individual himself."[19]

During Merton's early monastic writings, he stressed the importance of Catholic education, which to him at that time held an integral moral component that promoted and sustained a healthy faith-filled family unit. Although more of an atheist in his youth, Merton recalled the difference in attitude between the Catholic students of Saint Antonin, who exuded simplicity and affability in comparison to the violent, ill-tempered, and bullying students of Lycée, where he was schooled. Merton also specifically recalled a charitableness in the nephew of the Privats, a Catholic family Merton and his father boarded with while in Murat, France. Throughout *Seven Storey Mountain*, Merton's use of language portrays a bias toward Catholic education by applying only positive attributes throughout the recollections of his youth in the actions and behaviors of children who were schooled in Catholic educational settings, in comparison to the schoolboys of his school or his own behavior during his youth.[20]

His bias toward Catholic education seems to have waned toward the end of his life, though. In a response to Suzanne Butorovich, a Catholic high school student at the time, Merton wrote that if he were to change aspects of *Seven Storey Mountain*, in 1967, he would remove much of the overzealous support of Catholic schools.[21] Merton, unfortunately, did not elaborate

---

17. Del Prete, "Thomas Merton on Mark Van Doren," 16–18.

18. Distefano, "Dan Walsh's Influence on the Spirituality of Thomas Merton," 4–13.

19. Merton, "Learning to Live," 3.

20. Merton, *Seven Storey Mountain*, 63.

21. Merton, "Letter to Suzanne Butorovich, July 18, 1967," 310.

why he felt differently about those passages regarding Catholic schooling, but clearly his perspective and fervent advocacy for Catholic schools had changed since first writing his autobiography, twenty years previous.

Nevertheless, it is clear that the tenets that define Catholic education were deeply important to Merton. His spiritual maturation in Catholicism paralleled the expectations of Catholic education: the learning of doctrinal truths, engaging the liturgy, learning from the heroes of the faith, and developing an ethical order of moral living within the lens of Catholic tradition. Through his continuous reading of Catholic authors during his time at Columbia and Saint Bonaventure, as well as following the lives and examples of holy people such as Thérèse of Lisieux, Damian Molokai, and John Bosco, Merton zealously learned about the traditions and history of his newly professed spiritual beliefs.[22] Merton's journals also indicate his interest in stories and examples of the lives of the saints, such as John Vianney, and seeking inspiration through those that inspired him, such as the mysterious adolescent Roman martyr, Philomena.[23]

Adolescent Education: A Growth toward Unity in Self and with Others

The celebrated Italian educator Luigi Giussani stated that the body, mind, and spiritual development of a student has unique needs within their maturation and education.[24] As an adolescent matures, the education process ought to evolve into a dialogue between teacher and student from basic physical facts to a dialogue of the mind, and ultimately a communion of spirit; which is clearly demonstrated in the life of Merton within his relationships with Van Doren and Walsh.[25] This type of educational journey needs to be framed within a meaningful process of experiential verification and formation that will prompt the student to engage in healthy activities not because of duty, but their own initiative. The risk of adolescent education and maturation is that a student has to be offered the freedom to choose their own particular path or action by the instructor. This progresses

22. Merton, *Seven Storey Mountain*, 386.

23. Merton, *Journals of Thomas Merton*, 1:30.

24. See Giussani, *Risk of Education*.

25. See Del Prete, "Thomas Merton on Mark Van Doren," 16–18; Distefano, "Dan Walsh's Influence on the Spirituality of Thomas Merton," 4–13; and Daggy, "Editorial: Dan Walsh and Thomas Merton," 2.

beyond a calculable principle, but resides in a healthy balance of the need of the individual and the need of the community. "To educate means to help the human soul enter into the totality of the real."[26] It is only through real experiences that individuals exist in community together, and ultimately sheds light into the pinnacle example of community, the Trinity.

The education of the whole human person should be at the core of adolescent education. As mentioned previously, an individual learns to grow and thrive through the assistance and participation in community; likewise, the body grows as a whole not independently of other aspects of the body. That continuity of maturation is an essential element in being able to negotiate and engage the various challenges that affect one in life experiences. The dynamics of community and individual connectivity in the church has been a focus of the earliest written Christian documents (1 Cor 12; Eph 1:15–23).

An individual is born in existence from, and formed in the midst of, community.[27] To develop and flourish, an individual matures and comes to realize their full potential within a community, and contributes to the community through offering their talents for the needs of society. Before an individual understands their existence or responsibility in such a community, they are subject to a process of formation into a particular style of life through their education. This journey is not one that only consists of gaining knowledge, but the individual must allow that knowledge to influence their life and actions. The twenty-first century now presents new challenges regarding this view of education and the human interconnectivity. With the technological boom, new communities, new needs, and new forms of communication are defining human interaction. Merton briefly reflected on such changing perspectives in a poem which explored the dangers of predefined mechanical and humorless responses of a technological system that could one day control and determine the course of humanity:

CABLE #8

Write a prayer to a computer? But first of all you have to find out how It thinks. *Does It dig prayer?* More important still, does It dig me, and father, mother, etc., etc.? How does one begin: "O Thou great unalarmed and humorless electric sense . . ."? Start out wrong and you give instance offense. You may find yourself shipped off to

26. Giussani, *Risk of Education*, 105.

27. See Merton, *No Man Is an Island*; Merton, "Learning to Live," 3–24.

the camps in a freight car. Prayer is a virtue. But don't begin with the wrong number.[28]

Thus, education cannot be impartial or valueless; it depends upon dialoguing with authentic truths of experiential reality and humanity to lead a life of action and not a frozen passivity from fear and indecision. As Pope Francis stated to a group of Italian educators in 2014:

> Education cannot be neutral. It is either positive or negative; either it enriches or it impoverishes; either it enables a person to grow or it lessens, even corrupts him. The mission of schools is to develop a sense of truth, of what is good and beautiful. And this occurs through a rich path made up of many ingredients.[29]

Education: Application with Adolescents

In the climate of contemporary culture adolescents often feel anxious about how a misunderstood or distorted comment could lead to peer ridicule, labeling, and bullying.[30] To grow and mature into who they are called to be and recognize their purpose in life, adolescents need a safe environment to be able to mature mentally, physically, and spiritually. Self-discovery is therefore an essential search throughout adolescence. Through learning about personal preferences, an adolescent comes to know who they are and their purpose with much more clarity. Adolescent education should not only develop a sense of self-worth and dignity in catechesis and formation for an adolescent, but it needs to address and identify the need for self-worth and dignity in others.[31] The call for self-discovery and developing mature and healthy relationships with others is a theme consistently present throughout the writings of Thomas Merton.

Practical Examen: Questions for Reflection

- Have *I* limited the nature of education to merely standardized measures and neglected the importance of all of life's experiences?

28. Merton, "Cables to the Ace #8," 399–400.
29. Francis, "Address of Pope Francis to Students and Teachers," para. 6.
30. See Malewitz, "Who Am I? Why Am I Here?"
31. See Malewitz and Pacheco, "Living Solidarity," 324–32.

- Have *I* taken time to reflect on those personal experiences that have defined *my* life?

- Have *I* offered significant time to listen to and learn from meaningful experiences that define an adolescent's journey, so far in his or her life?

- Have *I* given an opportunity and helped an adolescent reflect on experiences that have defined his or her life?

- Thomas Merton had several teachers that helped define his life and perspective. Have *I* thought about those teachers who inspired real-life learning and what characteristics they possessed that were most admirable?

- Do *I* allow others to define my life and my actions? Have *I* been open to discover my true self?

4

Rituals

Engagement with Tradition

We must go to church and pray to the Saints and to Mary and to Christ our Lord that the blindness of sin be healed in us and we must first of all love and glorify them, and though we are full of sin, we must not be full of despair, but pray continually with humility and meekness for forgiveness of our sins and for increase in Love and Faith and Hope . . . The world is very unhappy and terrible now, but beyond it and in it and around it is still the Love and Mercy of God, that only waits for our prayers.[1]

ONE OF THE FIRST lifelong experiences of education, or self-discovery, is the experiences of patterns of action that may, or may not, bear deep emotional and symbolic meaning. Those repeated actions which convey deep and lasting meaning often become personal rituals. Such rituals come to define our future actions and responses, and offer a preparation on how to navigate and make sense of the world around us, and its meaning within our lives.

In early 1938, Merton was in the full swing of his conversion and started to consistently attend mass. It was during this period that he sought to be baptized into the Catholic Church. He was formally accepted into the church through baptism on November 16, 1938, and continued to zealously

1. Merton, *Journals of Thomas Merton*, 1:31.

develop his life of faith.[2] The quote above, from a journal entry roughly six months after his baptism, offers a clear example of how essential rituals were in his life at that time. Merton started a lifestyle based significantly on ritual. It was not just that he attended mass consistently, but his whole life started developing an evolving rhythm based on his newfound faith. Although he kept journals before his baptism, after his baptism he started fresh in his attentiveness of recording his thoughts.[3] As a reader explores Merton's cataloged journals, it becomes apparent that the connection of liturgical feast days begins to play a significant role in his thoughts and place within the church. Although initially occurring haphazardly, this ritual becomes much more consistent after he enters monastic life.[4] Likewise, the intercession of the saints also had an important influence for Merton, as he ritually dedicated or concluded his journals with JMJT or JMJBT throughout the 1940s.[5]

Such rituals for Merton should not be interpreted as superstition. They were a deep part of his internal dialogue, his search for authenticity, and a life dedicated to consistency in prayer and action. Much like an adolescent eager to learn all that he or she can about an area of interest to develop further skills or talents in a particular passion, such as music, athletics, theatre, or literature, Merton dove deeply into the spiritual example of the saints and traditions of the church.

Like Merton during this period, adolescents often search for new and meaningful role models that have struggled similar feats throughout their lives. They yearn for exemplars to emulate, learn, and grow from. To connect to such an exemplar, an adolescent will often attempt to embody enticing ideals, lifestyle, or creed which correspond to the stage of life that the adolescent is experiencing. The embodiment of passion, authenticity, and

---

2. Higgins, *Thomas Merton: Faithful Visionary*, 21.

3. Merton, *Journals of Thomas Merton*, 1:xi, xv.

4. The dating of Feast Days in Merton's journals seems to date back as early as October 4, 1939, but becomes much more consistent from 1942 and afterward; see *Journals of Thomas Merton*, vol. 1. Merton also directly used this scheme in *The Seven Storey Mountain* to highlight significant events in his life, but the connection to the Feast also seems to serve as a reminder and acknowledgment of the dependence on the presence of God throughout his life.

5. Similar to Fulton Sheen's familiar devotion of JMJ (Jesus, Mary, Joseph) which became the first written letters on his blackboard throughout *Life is Worth Living* (1952–57), throughout his journals in 1942 Merton concluded with JMJT (Jesus, Mary, Joseph, Thérèse) or used JMJBT (Jesus, Mary, Joseph, Bernard, Thérèse) in dedication to the Holy Family and the Saints. See Merton, *Journals of Thomas Merton*, 2:4–12, 15.

advocacy can often become a shibboleth for an adolescent when searching for an exemplar. Thomas Merton's life and writings can offer such an example as a real-life exemplar through the experiences of authentic self-discovery, passion, and advocacy found throughout his themes and writings. These aspects of self-discovery, or lived experience, might fuel the adolescent's ambitions and offer meaning to the adolescent in this stage of life, which ultimately manifests in an advocacy or drive in an adolescent for a particular passion or life purpose.

Examples of Adolescence Rituals

One of the great challenges of the contemporary culture, especially with adolescents, is needing to address the strong influence of pure empiricism or scientism: the belief that the only things that can be measurable by the senses have value or merit. One of the first lessons I consistently offer to adolescent students, when teaching a new semester of philosophy or theology, is to help guide the adolescents to reengage with the world beyond their mere senses. It is essential to have adolescents experience this lesson because many of them have been taught that only empirical facts are truth, and if something cannot be proven by facts, then it cannot be considered true. This lesson then usually evolves into a springboard to discuss rituals. A ritual is a tangible or measurable action or event, that bears a deep symbolic meaning. For the adolescents, it is easy to express the importance of an action but it is much more difficult to articulate why a particular action was assigned to a given a symbolic meaning in their lives.

Common rituals that adolescents often discuss throughout these lessons include actions such as receiving a driver's license or a class ring, attending dances and parties like prom, and graduation. Some adolescents have also discussed the importance of a first date, wearing a shirt or other piece of clothing that belongs to someone that they are dating, or even pet names. Although these actions seem ordinary, they are given emotional and symbolic significance for that individual, or group, or within a particular relationship or setting. There was much panic, pain, grief, and anxiety when the pandemic of 2020 postponed and cancelled many of these significant ritual activities for the senior class; just as many adults were anxious and lost when Christian rituals such as church services and mass were suspended.

With the technological boom, adolescents have also developed new rituals that have deep meaning and significance in their lives, such as sustaining a streak on Snapchat. A Snapchat streak refers to the consecutive number of days that two individuals reply to each other on the given application. This technological ritual has become a strong metric for many adolescents on the value, or real depth of the relationship with the other.[6] For personal anecdotal insight, I asked my youngest daughter, an adolescent, about her beliefs about Snapchat streaks, and she stated when she first started to use Snapchat, the length of the streak indicated the depth of commitment to that relationship, and when a steak ended, it felt like the end of that friendship. Although this may not seem clear to an adult, it is important to recognize and have a sense of the importance that such actions have in the life of an adolescent.

Unfortunately, contemporary adolescents often seem to have little engagement and understanding of traditional rituals.[7] Adolescence is a time where boundaries are tried and tested, and many previously taught traditions may be challenged by an adolescent; but that does not mean that adolescents do not long to be part of meaningful experiences. Through their exploration, adolescents search for experiences and rituals that give their life meaning, as well as an identity that can bring them pride and satisfaction.[8]

Fully functional and healthy adults are not born; they are made through being tested, through the experience of rituals, challenged, defined, and pushed into maturity.[9] Rituals have purpose and meaning. Initiation ceremonies bring an individual into a community. Susan Morris Shaffer and Linda Perlman Gordon, celebrated authors on the parenting of adolescents, stated that several coming-of-age rituals are present in other cultures, but clear rituals for adolescents seem to be lacking in contemporary America.[10] Leonard Sax, physician and adolescent psychologist, stated that there are very few geared rituals or celebrations, especially for young men, to honor the ascent to, and assent of, maturity which defines a healthy sense of adulthood.[11] Although there are rituals of passage, many are often negative such

---

6. Lorenz, "Teens Explain the World of Snapchat's Addictive Streaks."

7. See Dean, *Almost Christian*; Convey, *What Do Our Children Know About Their Faith?*

8. See Quinn, "Purposeful Explorers."

9. See Rohr and Martos, *From Wild Man to Wise Man*, 31–36.

10. Shaffer and Gordon, *Why Boys Don't Talk*; Shaffer and Gordon, *Why Girls Talk.*

11. Sax, *Boys Adrift.*

as: binge drinking at twenty-one (or before), peer celebrations of sexual activities, gang initiations, or fraternity hazings. Many of the remaining positive rituals have been changed by contemporary media for their regard of being antiquated, perpetuating ideologies, or gender-biased nature.

Rituals: Finding Meaning in Life and Tradition

Rituals offer tangible and meaningful reminders to relationships and our identity within those relationships. Although rituals are often commonplace, they can easily be taken for granted or become commercialized. Rituals within relationships such as anniversaries, gifts, or even Valentine's Day have changed from the primary focus on the importance of the individual and meaning of the relationship, to assigning a metric or value to the relationship through a monetary gift that serves as a token to demonstrate the meaning of the relationship. Contemporary adolescents now find themselves in a world of consistent measurement and judgment of the value of relationships based on material possessions and monetary status. This perspective has evolved into a social attention and, to some degree, objectification as adolescents use social media as an avenue of competition to prove the lengths they have gone monetarily to illustrate the love they have for their significant other, such as with posting elaborate Valentine's Day, Christmas gifts, or prom-posals.

Thomas Merton rightly challenged this notion of metric value by explaining authentic relationship with God: "The contemplative life isn't something objective that is 'there' and to watch, after fumbling around, you finally gain access. The contemplative life is a dimension of our subjective existence. Discovering the contemplative life is a new self-discovery."[12] Likewise, the experience of rituals is not an objective reality; the ritual meaning should engage and lead to discovery of the self through relationship with the other. So, understanding the importance of ritual flows directly from the journey of learning about ourselves. Without tangible and significant symbolic rituals within the life of the human person, one is left to be defined by the experiences of others without the opportunity to assess the essential contribution of their life with the other. It is through consistent meaningful activities that rituals develop and become traditions. These ceremonies then come to define a family, group, or organization based on the shared experience. These shared experiences help strengthen and deepen

12. Merton, "Contemplation in a World of Action," 340.

the relationship of the individual and the relationships with others within that same shared experience.

Christianity includes many traditional ritual practices. These rituals are highly symbolic and offer tangible expressions of faith within the transcendent realities of the religious perspective. For many adolescents, who may not fully understand the symbolism or belief in a transcendent reality, ritual can become sterile and meaningless. Within the Catholic tradition, there are many rituals that are used to help deepen and explain the faith through a tangible experience, such as mass, the sacraments, prayer devotions, novenas, iconography, and Lectio Divina. There are also many rituals that hold a sacred cultural significance such as a quinceañera, Las Posadas, fasting practices, and pilgrimages, that define and help discover new aspects of the self.

The current standards for the religious education curriculum for Catholic adolescents includes a catechetical and formational introduction to a collection of doctrinal elements for adolescents such as vocabulary, moral and ethical theory, as well as the incorporation of prayers and ritual experiences.[13] A holistic ministry for adolescents, though, should include, an introduction, explain, and promotion of the importance of the rituals, since it cannot be assumed that all adolescents have such an understanding.[14]

The National Catholic Education Association's (NCEA) national assessment of adolescent Catholic education, the ACRE exam, offers a comprehensive assessment of the knowledge and experience of students with rituals, like the sacraments. Religious education scholar and researcher John Convey's analysis of the ACRE data indicated that the sacraments are one of the misunderstood concepts in the secondary curriculum.[15] Many students do not remember their personal experiences of the sacraments nor do they frequent the liturgy enough to have consistent experiences of the sacraments in the community of the church. Without a tangible or consistent experience of the sacraments the course material on these holy actions have little meaning or connection to the life of an adolescent. Relating course material to a student's life and reality is an essential quality for twenty-first-century educational practice.[16]

13. *Doctrinal Elements of a Curriculum Framework*, 2008.

14. See Delgatto, *Catholic Youth Ministry*; and East et al., *Leadership for Catholic Youth Ministry*.

15. Convey, *What Do Our Children Know About Their Faith?*

16. John Paul II, "Catechesi Tradendae"; and Francis, "Evangelii Gaudium."

Merton, and the Need for Rituals for Grounding the Heart and Soul

Thomas Merton, as indicated above, was a man whose journey of self-discovery was based on rituals. The sacred actions and transcendent meanings of the symbolic rites became a grounded bridge between the world and the divine reality. For Merton, rituals were a tangible experience of grace that allowed the development of the self to come into greater union with the divine will of God.

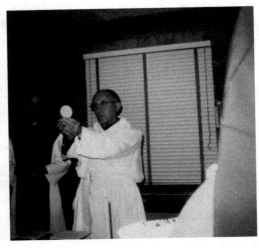

This union with God was experienced most tangibly by Merton through prayer. Merton was clear on the purpose of prayer: "Prayer then means yearning for the simple presence of God, for a personal understanding of his word, for knowledge of his will and for capacity to hear and obey him."[17] This ritual time with God, through prayer, should not be interpreted as an obligation or an action based out of fear of hell, but should be recognized as a fruit of a desire for an intimate relationship with God that brings to light the deepest and authentic desire of the heart and soul. It is no coincidence that Scripture continually relates Israel's relationship with God in the human terms of intimacy. Through the limited expression of human language, relationship with God is described in the most powerful concepts and metaphor of human desire and heartbreak: love (1 John); adultery (Amos); intimacy (Song); a wedding feast (John; Rev); and trust in the providence of God (Tob).[18]

There is also considerable evidence of Merton's devotion to Mary, which is demonstrated through his letters and especially his journals. Merton composed several prayers addressed to her seeking comfort, protection,

17. Merton, *Contemplative Prayer*, 45.

18. Merton was fascinated with the story of Tobit and explored the spiritual implications of the story, as documented in his journal. See October 24 and 26, 1940. Merton, *Journals of Thomas Merton*, 1:241–44.

and guidance.[19] This exploration finds continuity in the rituals and devotion of the Church that was leading up to encyclical "Marialis Cultus." The encyclical offers that through the liturgy, we can gain a glimpse into the inexpressible love Mary has for her son.[20] Through liturgical seasons, like Advent and Christmas, Pope Paul VI reminds the church how closely the liturgical seasons and our emotions tie together, and can be used to enhance our prayer through devotion and imitation of Mary. Through the help and imitation of Mary's life, one can gain a deeper involvement and spiritual connectedness to the liturgy of the word and find its fulfillment in the liturgy of the Eucharist. Through deep ritual expressions, Thomas Merton was an ordinary individual who was able to recognize deeper realities and write in such a way that evoked passion and desire within the spiritual ennui of the American culture. Without the rhythm of rituals, Merton argued one would be disconnected from their experience of the transcendence.

The grounding of the heart and soul does not come through extraordinary interventions during a relationship but subsists in the ordinary and routine rituals of everyday existence. This might be one of the reasons why the significance of rituals can be easily overlooked by adolescents; it is often assumed within the adolescent experience of extremes that deep and life-defining meaning comes from the most extraordinary aspects of one's life, while the everyday and commonplace is often neglected or taken for granted. It should not be so with rituals, though, as every sacred action bears an equally sacred meaning within the relationship, but most especially the identity of the individual through theological reflection.

Rituals: Application with Adolescents

Spiritual authors Richard Rohr and Joseph Martos state that there is a necessity of rituals in the maturation of an individual, especially males. Common rituals today for adolescents often surround athletics: making the team, practice, celebrations, and grief are frequent aspects of team life. As demonstrated in the letters of Paul of Tarsus, sports language and symbolism can offer a strong springboard for students unfamiliar with concepts of the body of Christ and offering one's gifts and talents for unity and the betterment of others (1 Cor 9:24–27).

---

19. Such as Merton, *Journals of Thomas Merton*, 1:409.
20. Paul VI, "Marialis Cultus," §4.

The sacraments have an essential role in the life of a Christian. These rituals bring an individual to a tangible presence of living God present in our lives. They strengthen and make holy the recipient to recognize and contribute their part of the body of Christ, as well as give worship to God.[21] How many students, or adults for that matter, understand the depth that is the gift of the sacraments? Many adolescents will likely know or recognize the names of the sacraments: baptism, confirmation, Eucharist, reconciliation, anointing of the sick, holy orders, and matrimony, but that is not something that a religious educator can take for granted in Catholic schools today. Few students will have an idea of symbols associated with the sacraments, and very few may have any sense of the deeper reality of the gift of grace that is present such moments.

Media Examples for Adolescents

The following examples, based on films, can offer adolescents a deeper sense of the power of symbols and themes to invite a dialogue of the purpose and belief of rituals within the church and their lives. Unfortunately, there is not enough opportunity to offer a suggestion for every ritual. Hopefully these three ideas will offer a starting point to explore further applications. The following examples are topics that I have used in the past that have engaged adolescents to explore and engage a world beyond mere empirical sense to start to gain a better grasp of the importance of rituals in their lives.

Black[22]

This 2005 award-winning Bollywood film offers a contemporary retelling of Helen Keller's story, which was originally enshrined through the 1962 film *The Miracle Worker*. As was the case with its predecessor, the engagement and comprehension of water becomes the catalyst for the deaf-blind adolescent, Michelle, to engage and begin to understand the world around her, as a baptism to a new world. As the film progresses, though, it is evident that as Michelle matures in a holistic development, her teacher, Debraj, begins to slowly lose his understanding of the world, through the development of Alzheimer's disease. The film explores the concept of the journey of

---

21. Paul VI, "Sacrosanctum Concilium," §59.
22. Bhansali, *Black*.

how the student becomes the teacher, and how the teacher, the student; as well as why that relationship in community is essential to the discovery of one's authentic self. The film includes a beautiful use of cinematography to contrast light and darkness which parallels the comprehension of authentic knowledge and holistic growth and confusion, and as well as meaningful routines, rituals, throughout the lives of the family and the teacher.

Throughout the course of the film, water directly parallels the spiritual experience of baptism in the church, opening the floodgates to reception into the world and community. The visual reoccurrence of water establishes the importance of the ritual of flowing water as a tangible experience which carries a deeper reality of cleansing, connection, and an entrance into a new reality. Through the examples of symbolic nature of water, light, and clothing in the film, adolescents can compare and examine the liturgical rituals of the sacrament of baptism through the bridge of a narrative native to their culture.

"Guru of Go"[23]

This 2010 ESPN 30-for-30 documentary focuses on the ups and downs throughout the career of celebrated basketball coach Paul Westhead. Westhead, whose basketball style was dubbed "the system," pushed his players to the extreme of their limits of endurance and consistently utilized a fastbreak style of play to shoot more points than the opposing team. Through this style of play Westhead won a NBA title with the Los Angeles Lakers in 1980 as well as a WNBA championship in 2007. Between 1985 and 1990, though, Westhead coached men's collegiate basketball at Loyola Marymount. Tragedy struck on March 4, 1990, when Westhead's forward and one of the NCAA's Division I star athletes, Hank Gathers, died on the court from cardiac arrest. The documentary reflects on the sudden and traumatic experience of Hank's death by the Loyola Marymount team and also highlights the importance of rituals as the team tried to regain stability in their volatile grief.

An example of such ritual shown through the documentary was demonstrated by Gathers's close friend, Bo Kimble, who decided to throw his first free-throw shot left-handed in honor of and mirroring his deceased friend. This symbol became a consistent ritual for Kimble, as he continued to shoot each first free-throw left-handed throughout the college

23. Couturié, "Guru of Go."

tournament that year.[24] This ritual became a reminder of the presence, as well as a ritual sign of hope, for Bo and the fans of Loyola Marymount. For adolescents the sign, symbol, or gesture done in remembrance of a friend or revered hero who died can create a deep connection and remembrance of the relationship with that individual. This line of discussion can develop into an avenue to discuss the meaning and emotions of liturgical rituals, such as the final movements and actions surrounding the Last Supper between Jesus and his apostles leading up to his horrific death.

Doctor Strange[25]

The 2016 Marvel film *Doctor Strange* offers a glimpse into Hollywood's take on trying to negotiate the existence of transcendent reality. Dr. Stephen Strange, an egotistic but highly accomplished neurosurgeon, experiences a life-altering accident that critically injures his hands and destroys his conceived purpose of life, leaving him debilitated. In his search to regain his purpose, he travels to a mysterious monastery and is introduced to life beyond a mere empirical reality. Over the course of the film, Strange is challenged with various temptations and desires throughout the journey of finding his authentic self. His journey is grounded on the need for understanding and engaging with rituals, sacred actions, that involve time and space and ultimately are defined within *kairos*. In his review of *Doctor Strange*, Bishop Robert Barron stated that the film offered a clear and well-depicted example of Hollywood offering a credible acknowledgment of metaphysical realities that is often ridiculed in modern culture.[26]

This film offers a powerful example for adolescents to recognize and engage with the tangible and transcendent realities that exist around them. Through reflection questions that challenge adolescents to find similarities between characters and objects of the film with Scripture they can begin to connect the dots to the deeper truths of symbols and rituals in Christianity, such as the roles of sacramentals, prayers, and meditation.

24. Kimble, "Hank."
25. Derrickson, *Doctor Strange.*
26. Barron, "Bishop Barron on 'Doctor Strange.'"

Practical Examen: Questions for Reflection

- What rituals, or ritual actions, hold a sacred meaning throughout *my* life?

- Have *I* shared the history or importance of these rituals, or ritual actions, with someone else, such as a spouse or child?

- Have *I* created opportunities for an adolescent to experience and learn the meaning of personal and traditional rituals?

- Do *I* communicate clearly and well with adolescents about the importance of the physical and metaphysical realities within a ritual?

- Have *I* explored the importance of contemporary trending rituals within society, through common trends in television shows, films, or social media, especially with adolescents?

- Have *I* given an adolescent the time and opportunity to share and explain some of his or her most valued rituals with me or others?

5

Silence

Closing the Mouth, Opening the Heart and Mind

Those who love their own noise are impatient of everything else . . . It is the silence of the world that is real. Our noise, our business, our purposes, and all our fatuous statements about our purposes, our business, and our noise: these are the illusion.[1]

THOMAS MERTON OFFERED A deep and penetrating understanding of the difference between reality and those superficial aspects that compose our world. This is not a concept that is easy for an adult to understand, so why should we assume that it is important for an adolescent? Or that it is even possible for an adolescent to experience the depth of this reality? As mentioned previously, Merton did not distinguish the needs of an adolescent as being completely different than that of a young adult. He treated both with equal honesty and straightforwardness. The search for balance, order, rhythm, and harmony, which ultimately brings happiness, is essential for all human flourishing.[2]

But how can one find that happiness without listening to God, the creator of that happiness? To truly listen to God, Thomas Merton indicated that an individual would need to have a relationship with God. A

---

1. Merton, *No Man Is an Island*, 257.
2. Merton, *No Man Is an Island*, 127.

relationship develops through rituals, time, attention, but with God silence is also essential to cultivate such a relationship. Like the rhythm and balance of any healthy relationship, there is a necessary time to speak and time to listen; to grow, learn, and mature in communion with the other. Although God does not manifest divine presence in a clear and tangible way, such as in our relationships with colleagues, friends, and family, God is present, and can be heard, through the heart of an individual. Merton explained further: "By 'prayer of the heart' we seek God himself present in the depths of our being and meet him there by invoking the name of Jesus in faith, wonder and love."[3] This union in intimacy depends on our ability to be open to God, and be sure that one's heart and mind is not already so full that there is no room.

The On-the-Go Adolescent Lifestyle

The contemporary climate of adolescents is one that seems to be consistently on the go. From morning to night, adolescent students often experience demands for their attentiveness at school, practice, athletic games, social media presence, and many other expectations, like at a job or a work site. There is little to no opportunity for peaceful rest within the busy schedule of a twenty-first-century adolescent. Adolescents can easily feel torn in multiple directions and can often feel at a complete loss regarding how and why their time has passed. It is important for adolescents to reclaim their time and live purposefully through meaningful actions that become defining experiences. Here, Thomas Merton's wisdom can become monumental in that struggle throughout the search for meaning and identity.

In the documentary *Race to Nowhere*, which explores the consequences regarding the stress and anxiety of adolescent life within the high-stakes American achievement culture, educational researchers Vicki Abeles and Jessica Congdon keenly illustrated that many contemporary adolescents feel burned out, depressed, disengaged, and can develop stress-related illnesses from the pressures placed upon their lives.[4] Some of the stressors mentioned throughout the documentary included family expectations, high expectations from coaches or club directors, college admissions and placement exams, and the total lack of downtime available to find rest or relaxation throughout the

3. Merton, *Contemplative Prayer*, 6.

4. See Abeles and Congdon, *Race to Nowhere*; and Abeles and Rubenstein, *Beyond Measure*.

school year. This consistent need for energy and escape has created the environment for many adolescents to seek relief through an overindulgence of energy drinks, alcohol, vaping, and other drugs.

Through her research on the exhausted spirit of contemporary adults, biochemist and renowned nutritional speaker Libby Weaver indicated that the following were consistent trends that led to low energy: lack of or poor sleeping patterns, toxic or processed foods, lack of sunlight, stress, studying, money worries, boredom, not having enough personal time, and having no purpose in life.[5] These physical and psychological challenges can have significant affects in the ability to form and sustain healthy engagement with peers and colleagues. Although these trends were found in adult participants, an on-the-go adolescent lifestyle could easily parallel such experiences, or have even more severe experiences due to the physiological stage of life of the adolescent.

Walter Brueggemann, scriptural exegete and theologian, adds further insight when this concept is examined from a spiritual perspective. Brueggemann explained that the concept of Sabbath, based on the perspective of the revered twentieth-century rabbi Abraham Heschel, is bound by the concept of peaceful rest within a time of devotion. Based on the roots of the creation story in Genesis, Sabbath is part of the natural order of human creation and flourishing. Brueggemann contended that: "Sabbath-keeping is a way of making a statement of particular identity amid a larger public identity of maintaining and enacting a counter-identity that refuses 'mainstream' identity, which itself entails an anti-human practice and the worship of anti-human gods."[6] Here Brueggemann spiritually challenged that without proper rest and time with God, we cannot be authentically human.

Merton: On the Need for Retreat and Rest

> If the contemplative orientation of prayer is its emptiness, its "uselessness," its purity, then we can say that prayer tends to lose its true character in so far as it becomes busy, full of ulterior purposes, and committed to programs that are beneath its own level.[7]

These words of Thomas Merton cut the culture to the quick. Here Merton directly indicated that prayer, relationship with God, is useless to

5. Weaver, *Exhausted to Energized*, 6–7.

6. Brueggemann, *Sabbath as Resistance*, 21.

7. Merton, *Contemplative Prayer*, 92.

the mainstream culture that is focused on commodity, materialism, and monetary growth. For an adolescent, the goods of secular society are extremely alluring. Fame, wealth, power, and pleasure are consistently promoted on the television, film, and the internet. How can the words of a prophetic hermit reach beyond the bombastic noise of the surrounding culture? It is first essential for adolescents to experience the difference between noise and silence.

Through a more poetic medium Merton reflected how one's very nature is bound to the essential nature of silence:

IN SILENCE (excerpt: stanzas 1 and 2)

Be still
Listen to the stones of the wall.
Be silent, then try
To speak your

Name.
Listen
To the living walls.
Who are you?
Who
Are you? Whose
Silence are you?[8]

Through the use of such pauses and phrasing in his poetry Merton deliberately set the stage for the reader to purposefully slow down and be one with the present moment, the present reflection of personal thought; as if it were through the deliberate silence that one can hear the depths of their purpose and calling.

As is clear, though, Merton did not assume that resting in silence was an easy task. It is through the silence that one

8. Merton, "In Silence," 280.

meets the consuming fire of the Spirit which refines, proves, and removes the personal masks of all that is false within ourselves which has developed and become our assumed identity throughout life. In the previous picture of Merton kneeling on his ordination day, coincidentally is bathed in the light and silence of Gethsemani; becoming ignited with Spirit. He concluded the same poem by stating:

IN SILENCE (excerpt: stanza 4)

"I will try, like them
To be my own silence:
And this is difficult. The whole
World is secretly on fire. The stones
Burn, even the stones
They burn me. How can a man be still or
Listen to all things burning? How can he dare
To sit with them when
All their silence
Is on fire?"[9]

Calming the Heart and Mind: Through the Words and Experiences of Adolescents

A growing trend utilized by teachers to assist with classroom management is the practice of meditation, to help students find balance and offer a sense of calm and center their life.[10] Retreat and wellness centers have started offering courses and certifications specifically designed for educators to learn how to introduce meditation into their classrooms and help students find peace and balance from the stress in their lives. With these insights in mind, I incorporated a silent meditation as one of the activities of the exploratory curriculum.

Thomas Merton stated: "[We] cannot understand the true value of silence unless [we have] a real respect for the validity of language, for the reality which is expressible in language is found, face to face and without medium, in silence."[11] Using Merton's insight, I introduced the adolescents

9. Merton, "In Silence," 281.

10. See Mata, "Meditation," 109–19; Zinger, "Educating for Tolerance and Compassion," 25–28.

11. Merton, Thoughts in Solitude, 114.

to silence through an eight-minute short film, "Noise."[12] This short film, from a series of short topical multimedia theological reflections by author and speaker Rob Bell, challenges the viewer to reflect on the purpose of silence, from a Scriptural perspective. It is comprised of introductory dialogue that explains the bombardment of noise that has come to define our contemporary world, then contains roughly six minutes of Scripture passages for the viewer to read in silence. The clip was used as a conversation starter to help the students develop language and discuss a brief experience before a longer silent meditation, as well as an opportunity to verbally reflect as a large group on centering one's self. The students later wrote personal reflections on their longer silent meditative experience through personal journaling the day following the silent meditation.

The following narrative vignettes serve as supporting evidence of the aesthetic engagement of the adolescents by demonstrating sensory, logical, emotional, and ethical connections expressed by the students throughout the lesson of the session. I invited the students to openly dialogue and share their experiences of silence as well as their feelings of the reflection on the topic of silence. This initial dialogue of the video clip on silence offered a range of interpretations and shared experiences from the student-participants:

> Jerome [verbal response; normal volume but collecting his thoughts]: you never really fully experience, like, real silence in the world because technology and stuff is your main focus and we never really take a minute to just be silent for awhile [sic], and be yourself.[13]

> Timothy [verbal response; soft volume, a bit anxious]: I think that sometimes you will get uncomfortable when you're, like, not saying anything, so you'll, like, fill the void and do something to lighten the mood and just leave the discomfort of not being able to hear anything.[14]

> Donald [verbal response; normal volume, clear]: silence represents the unknown, you don't know what or who it is sometimes.[15]

12. Stoner, "Noise."

13. Large group discussion, April 19, 2018.

14. Large group discussion, April 19, 2018.

15. Large group discussion, April 19, 2018.

To create a contrast between silence and noise, the conclusion of the short film, "Noise," incorporates a dramatic change from the six-minute silent reflection to a loud, bombastic, but incoherent noise. This cacophony of noise mirrors an individual flipping through TV channels but not stopping long enough to distinctly understand any of the dialogue on the television. The following vignette recounts a sequential conversation that specifically related to the adolescents' reactions to the dramatic change from silence to noise that occurred at the conclusion of the short film:

> Oakland [verbal response; normal volume but collecting his thoughts]: I kinda had my eyes closed and I was kinda drifting off a little bit. I wasn't falling asleep, but you know, it's like
>
> Robert [verbal response; sarcastically, seriously believing that Oakland fell asleep]: come on, Oakland.
>
> Oakland [normal volume but collecting his thoughts]: yea, but then I heard it and it shook me and it was like . . .
>
> Matthew [soft volume, passionate, cutting off Oakland before he finished]: that's kinda the way I felt—agitated. I was feeling calm and then felt agitated
>
> Harold [normal volume, frank, full eye contact]: Well I was like, I was kinda relieved cause, like, the silence can be kind of unnerving at times and, like, you really need the sound, you know.[16]

The following day, for the longer experience of silence, I purposefully decided to have the silent meditation experience occur in an unfamiliar part of the school grounds; a quiet part of the school that the students do not use or visit, a loft located above the student chapel:

> Above the student chapel there is a loft; it was originally designed to be a choir loft but was later renovated, with carpeting, to be a quiet place for students to meditate or reflect. Some of the junior and senior theology teachers use it, but it is rarely used by freshmen theology teachers. The walls are wood paneling and radiate a smell of an old cabin. As the students entered the space, they were excited to grab a cushion and find a comfortable spot to sit. Most of the students tried to sit along the side walls of the chapel, for back support. Each student found a spot to sit—they spread out—and had enough room to not touch other students. In the tradition of Christian practice, I struck a match—*whisk*—and lit a

16. Large group discussion, April 19, 2018.

candle; the candle offered little light but was a remembrance of the presence of Jesus for that moment and activity. I first brought the students into a posture proper for meditation: sitting with their backs straight. I also invited them to close their eyes and sit—in silence—focusing on their breathing—slow breathing: in and out—some students put their hand on their stomach to feel the expansion and deflation of the air, as a form of centering. I started by ringing a Tibetan singing bowl—the silent meditation began . . . the students sat quietly, a few squirmed, a couple needed to reposition their posture . . . if there was a noise, I would re-center the students on their breathing, slowly and softy recollecting their posture during the experience. As the time progressed most of the students remained silent—a couple of students feel asleep, one student started snoring and I had to gently nudge him to recollect his posture and presence to the activity. As the meditation drew closer to fifteen minutes, I noticed that there was much more squirming and louder movements. Because of the consistent fidgeting that was developing, I decided to shorten the silent meditation to sixteen minutes instead of twenty minutes to keep the intensity of the experience for the students' reflections.

When the students returned to the classroom, they were given roughly ten to fifteen minutes to personally reflect on their meditative experience using open-ended questions on their worksheets; their written answers were to be written on the blank lined page located on the back side of the worksheet. The adolescents' experiences consistently mentioned a feeling of calm, peace, and stillness in body and mind. Some of the adolescents even expressed a feeling of a lifting or removing of stress or pressure:[17]

> Harold: I felt peaceful during the meditation. This was the first time in a long time that I felt truly calm and safe. I would totally do this again because it helped me to relax and not be stressed. I liked the feeling of peace, healing, and safety I got from this.
>
> Richard: During the experience, I felt relaxed and I enjoyed it, overall. I wish we could do that for the whole day . . . It was a very good stress reliever.
>
> Robert: I feel really relieved of my stress. I never have a time where I can just sit still and think . . . I was able to get in a nice state of mind.
>
> Jerry: During the experience I felt very relaxed and in my element. I felt like I was in solitude, but not alone at the same time . . . I

17. Collected artifacts: worksheet, April 20, 2018.

meditate on my own occasionally, it's a truly different experience every time. The one core element is blissful physical relaxation and ease . . . I suffer from Derealization disorder, a condition where you feel like you're outside your body and that nothing is real. When this happens to me the only way to really help it is meditation or meditative breathing. The mind is a powerful tool and needs to be working properly all the time. This simple breathing can set my entire mind back on track, in just a few minutes.

Matthew: The mediation this week was very helpful to me. I was having major anxiety over personal stress . . . It helped me to center myself. I got to let go of what was holding me back.

Donald: During the meditation I felt at peace. I felt like my body was still and I had no burden on my back. If I wanted to move I moved slowly, like I was floating in water or gel . . . Yes, I would like to meditate again. I felt good and weightless, and my mind was clear.

Oakland: I felt very relaxed and not as stressed. The tests I have soon didn't seem as bad as I thought they were. I felt almost lighter; I felt like a weight was lifted off of me. I wish I was able to meditate for more time because I felt so relaxed.

A few of the student-participant responses indicated that they had varying types of engagement and interpretative experiences, such as falling asleep, anxiety to the stillness, and the inability to settle their thoughts:[18]

Steve: I don't feel like I was able to still my mind at all but it was good. It was a little discomforting.

Brad: During the experience I fealt [sic] relaxed and I fell asleep a couple of times but it was very peaceful.

Larry: I found it very hard to still my mind. Throughout the experience, I thought of a lot of things and found it sort of difficult to focus. I would like to meditate more because I think that it helps relieve stress, calm yourself, and overall, prepare your mind for what you will do next.

The students also indicated that silence is an unnerving and unfamiliar experience. As indicated above, Timothy expressed anxiety from his initial experience of silence: "I think that sometimes you will get uncomfortable

18. Collected artifacts: worksheet, April 20, 2018.

when you're . . . not saying anything, so you'll . . . fill the void."[19] When exploring the topic of balance there were three themes that emerged from the written data and dialogue transcriptions of the adolescent students:

1. silence is often unnerving and uncomfortable

2. rest is something that adolescents long for, and

3. meditation helped relieve stress.

After the experience of the meditation, many of the students felt a sense of calm and peace. For many of the students this settled awareness and silence allowed them to rest without the pressure of continual intellectual or athletic expectations. After the silent meditation Harold reflected on a longing for rest: "I felt peaceful during the meditation. This was the first time in a long time that I felt truly calm and safe."[20] In addition to the needed rest, many students also felt the relief from the continual stressors in their life. Through his written reflection, Matthew interpreted that the meditation was a source of peace: "The mediation this week was very helpful to me. I was having major anxiety over personal stress . . . It helped me to center myself. I got to let go of what was holding me back."[21]

Theologically, these themes have deep connection with two core aspects of Judeo-Christian beliefs: prayer and Sabbath. The Catechism of the Catholic Church states that prayer is: "a living relationship of the children of God with their Father who is good beyond measure, with his Son Jesus Christ and with the Holy Spirit."[22] Catholic radio personality and author Teresa Tomeo stated that it is the persistent noise in the world that limits the Christian's ability to hear God in their life.[23] The adolescents honestly shared the challenge of being silent, in a world of noise. One student claimed for him that silence represents the unknown, which is something he found unnerving. In a theological perspective, the consistency of the student responses of anxiety and the uncomfortable nature of sitting and reflecting in silence indicates that students feel more comfortable speaking without listening, and sharing without comprehending the context in which they are present.

19. Large group discussion, April 19, 2018.

20. Collected artifacts: worksheet, April 20, 2018

21. Collected artifacts: worksheet, April 20, 2018

22. *Catechism of the Catholic Church*, §2565.

23. See Tomeo, *Noise*.

The responses of the adolescents that indicate a desire of peace and calm suggest, like Tomeo indicated, adolescents do not know how to easily settle themselves to find stillness and relationship through prayer with God. The scholarship of Kenda Creasy Dean also supported that adolescents are more likely to talk at God or want God to answer their prayers, or wishlist, than settle themselves into a dialogue in prayerful relationship with God.[24] This data poses further questions regarding adolescents and their experiences of prayer and listening to God which cannot be addressed with great depth here but should be further researched.

A second theological theme that emerged from the writing and experiences of the students relates to the concept of Sabbath; not just as a day specifically reserved for rest in God, but a cyclic idea of healthily resting of the whole body. Throughout the collected responses, several students interpreted that they felt relaxed and that a weight was lifted during the silent meditative experience. As the body receives proper amounts of rest, it allows the whole human person, body, mind, and spirit to recollect energy, heal, and relieve anxiety.

When adolescents do not take time to allow their bodies to have proper rest, they will not be healthy holistically in body, mind, and spirit. The students interpreted that rest is an important aspect of their life that is lacking in various degrees. As the adolescent students indicated through their language: being "in my element," "feeling of peace, healing and safety I got from this," and "I felt like my body was still and I had no burden on my back," there was a holistic experience in body, mind, and spirit that the students interpreted and would like to experience again. These student comments also seem to echo the famous perspective of seeking for the whole and divine *telos* of the human person based in the ancient Christian claim of Augustine of Hippo: *cor nostrum inquietum est donec requiescat in Te*; our hearts are restless until they rest in You.[25] Merton echoed Augustine when describing the power of resting in the presence of God through monastic meditation, *oratio*, prayer, and contemplation.[26] Through these ancient practices, Merton claimed that one's heart is renewed by the Holy Spirit and centers on the essential nature of being. Through these prayers of the heart, the individual is renewed and finds strength.

---

24. See Dean, *Almost Christian.*

25. Augustine, *Conf.* 3.

26. See Merton, *Contemplative Prayer.*

Practical Examen: Questions for Reflection

- Have *I* taken time to sit in silence to merely listen for God?

- Am *I* aware of where my time is used throughout the day?

- Have *I* created opportunities for an adolescent to rest and be at peace, without feeling pressure or expectations?

- Do *I* communicate, with adolescents, the importance of seeking balance and a proper amount of rest?

- Have *I* been so eager to succeed that work and achievements have become more important than time given to my most significant relationships?

- Have *I* given, or supported, an adolescent when they have the opportunity to resist the pressure of society or peer groups to always be on the go?

6

True/False Self

Refining the Search for Authenticity

All sin starts from the assumption that my false self, the self that exists only in my own egocentric desires, is the fundamental reality of life to which everything else in the universe is ordered.[1]

A COMMON TREND TODAY with adolescents focuses on the importance of acknowledging the respect of one's identity and being your true, or authentic, self. It is an essential part of human nature to desire to discover one's true self, but few people believe that they have the luxury and the amount of time needed to reflect and discern the deepest aspects of their core being; it takes considerable effort and patience. Adolescents, although desiring acceptance in their wholeness and authenticity, often feel judged, labeled, and defined by external structures, such as family, school, the church, or through social media feedback. The desire to live authentically is not a new focus for contemporary adolescents; the search for authenticity is a deep human longing stronger than a contemporary trend. In the quote above, Merton directly acknowledged the importance of living one's true self and its nature and goodness, in comparison to the disorders of the good that manifest by habitually embodying the characteristics of the mask of the false self.

1. Merton, *New Seeds of Contemplation*, 34.

From the beginning of the first lines of his spiritual autobiography, *The Seven Storey Mountain*, Thomas Merton showcased his calling as a poet through the use of language, his deep conviction of faith, and in some sense illustrated an honest soul caught in a powerful struggle. This human struggle, through its genuine and authentic writing, parallels that of Augustine of Hippo,[2] and draws the reader into the view of a deeper reality of one's whole self and the reality of one's relationship with the world. Although I have often wondered how Augustine's *Confessions* were originally received by his contemporaries, we do know that Merton's spiritual autobiography became an unexpected success, catapulting a reclusive monk into the status of a celebrated author within religious and secular circles in the late 1940s.[3] The following picture shows Merton signing autographs for a group of the Little Sisters of the Poor, in the 1950s.

His spiritual autobiography became a voice longed for by a generation searching for meaning, dignity, and their own calling. From the perspective of an honest search for authenticity, Merton's writings realistically engaged and related to the struggles of the imperfect decisions and passions associated with a developing adolescent spiritual maturation.

2. Merton recorded in one of his earliest journal entries, May 2, 1939, his admiration of Augustine's *Confessions*; especially Book VII, Chapter 12, which focuses on the nature of the inherent goodness of creation. Brother Patrick Hart, in the commentary about that entry, mentioned that Merton's admiration of Augustine may have influenced *The Seven Storey Mountain*. I would argue that this admiration may have also helped pave the way of Merton's perspective on the dignity of humanity found throughout his writings. See Merton, *Journals of Thomas Merton*, 1:3. In a later entry Merton compares Augustine's *Confessions* with Rousseau's *Confessions*. Merton praises Augustine for focusing on God, not focusing on proclaiming the greatness of the human author as Rousseau did. Merton concluded by stating: "Confessions are only valid (in literature) if they confess God." Merton, *Journals of Thomas Merton*, 1:21. Merton's own confessions in *The Seven Storey Mountain* deliberately focus on the work of God, instead of himself as the sole protagonist.

3. See Higgins, *Thomas Merton: Faithful Visionary*, 29–32.

Adolescence and a Desire for Authenticity

Adolescents are at a stage of life where they struggle for a holistic identity, between the search for an authentic inner perception of their true self and the external identity formed through communal relationships and impressions of others. They exude passion and desire stability; they seek mystery but want to prove the secrets of the mystery with tangible facts; they long for acceptance but depend on labels to classify similarities and differences with others—the age of adolescence is not easy to negotiate. Kenda Creasy Dean and Brandy Quinn, scholars on adolescent spirituality, both indicated that this stage of life is a struggle for identity in the midst of intimacy and passion, acceptance, self-discovery, and advocacy.[4] The negotiation of feelings at this stage of life is complicated, and may not easily be understood by individuals who do not experience the same biological and hormonal releases of individuals during adolescence.

In Alfred Lord Tennyson's classic work "Ulysses," it was stated: "that which we are, we are—one equal temper of heroic hearts, made weak by time and fate, but strong in will to strive, to seek, to find, and not to yield."[5] When we strive in this journey of self-discovery to follow Christ and progress in more communion with the Spirit in life, it is more likely than not that an arduous journey will occur, but along that path there will be moments of divine grace. Thomas Merton acknowledged this journey and experience through his decision and declaration: "Father . . . I want to give God everything."[6]

Walter Brueggemann, theologian and Scripture scholar, in an article addressing human vocations, challenged: "Faith means to place ourselves in that vortex where life is granted, received, and risked."[7] An individual must risk to lose the notions of the self, through a human lens, and trust in God's plan to develop spiritually.

Musician and spiritual seeker Leonard Cohen stated similar thoughts in a documentary interview about his life and experiences: "Sometimes when you no longer see yourself as the hero of your own drama—expecting victory after victory, and you understand deeply that this is not

---

4. See Dean, *Almost Christian*; and Quinn, "Purposeful Explorers."

5. See Tennyson's "Ulysses," ll. 67–70, in Tennyson, *Complete Alfred Lord Tennyson*, 850–51.

6. Merton, *Seven Storey Mountain*, 401.

7. Brueggemann, "Covenanting as a Human Vocation," 128.

paradise . . . things become a lot easier."[8] For some, like Merton in *The Seven Storey Mountain*, this can happen through a maturation in their emotional, intellectual, and sexual development, while for others God may just bypass a progression and act through just one moment, as in the divine moment of conversion of Paul of Tarsus (Acts 9:1–19). Without taking the time to listen with patience and respond wholeheartedly, though, it is easy to miss the whole point of conversion, Christ's call for us to be closer to him; as the words of John the Baptist were attributed: "He must increase; I must decrease" (John 3:30).

Adolescence: The Roots of Christian Maturity

"We do not want to be beginners. But let us be convinced of the fact that we will never be anything else but beginners, all our life!"[9] Thomas Merton reminded his readers that contemplative prayer is a process of consistently learning and living the most elementary aspects of relationship with God. In this sense, Christian maturity could be considered the continual conversion process through which an individual conforms his, or her, life choices to imitate the image of Jesus, the New Adam, more than the image of the original Adam, from the dawn of creation. It is this spiritual dimension that matures in parallel with the physical and mental growth, where depending on how much one nurtures the spiritual life, they would grow closer to living their true vocation.

As a child, the spiritual life is one of greater dependence upon the faith of parents or guardians rather than one's own claimed faith. During adolescence it often seems as though the claiming of faith is a battle, where for every action there is an opposite and equal reaction through the risk of testing and trying boundaries to engage a personal faith. Throughout this risky process, there is always the possibility, and choice, to continue or give up if the challenge seems too difficult to surmount; as a child when first learning to ride a bicycle alone without the use of training wheels. Sometimes the challenge and principle is understood and embodied, while at other times an adolescent will get distracted with other objects, temptations, and poor choices and lose their spiritual balance, and fall again, assuming the mask of their false selves. It is through this process of Christian maturity that an

8. Lunson, *Leonard Cohen: I'm Your Man*, 11:15–11:45.

9. Merton, *Contemplative Prayer*, 13.

adolescent can seek and engage the Truth, which will ultimately illuminate their depth of purpose and give sight into their vocation.

Unlike physical or mental development, Christian maturity does not necessarily come as naturally. Through the influence of an empirical world and its influence, an individual's spiritual life has the possibility of remaining dormant, malformed, or neglected for an extended period of time. But as in the cases of Paul of Tarsus, Augustine of Hippo, and Thomas Merton, there was a point through a catalyst that the spark of the Spirit was so present that it was impossibly difficult to deny. Throughout this conversion experience, each of these exemplars became intrigued and fascinated to understand, find conviction, and live in and for that Truth, and to praise and proclaim that Truth with wholeheartedness.

With a similar call to understand the development of adolescents and their spiritual challenges, Kenda Creasy Dean indicated that true evangelization should not rely on only positive or joy-filled moments of life, but should also be found through reflecting on experiences of suffering, sacrifice, and all of the ups and downs of the gambit of human relationship. She charged ministers of adolescents to translate a witness of faith for further generations by modeling faithful behavior in all of life's circumstances. Dean brilliantly exemplified her point by stating that adults need to lead the way and to show adolescents how to live like Christ.[10] The best witness of the gospel message for an adolescent is through faithful action, without concern of fear or ridicule. Adolescents yearn for authentic witnesses and can easily spot hypocrisy; and through their passion can quickly become disillusioned and disheartened by hypocritical lifestyles, especially when associated with religious contexts.

"Christianity, if false, is of no importance, and if true, of infinite importance. The only thing it cannot be is moderately important."[11] Parents, and ministers, of adolescents, through their actions, must indicate the importance of faith in their honest witness which will be seen and acknowledged by youth. Thomas Merton did not hide, deny, or negate his faith when communicating with adolescents but offered a transparent witness of the importance of faith in his life and encouraged them to always be open to the importance of that joy of the gospel in their lives. Time is the currency that often speaks more than anything else. The amount of time one puts into a relationship can measure how important that relationship is to

10. Dean, *Almost Christian*, 121–23.

11. Dean, *Almost Christian*, 43.

the other person. How much time do adults spend authentically dialoguing with adolescents in comparison to individual activities such as watching television, using technology such as a computer or mobile device, or relaxing apart from others? A child can learn very quickly how important their relationship is from the amount of time devoted to that activity.

In *Renewing the Vision*, the USCCB offered a comprehensive framework that can offer a guide for ministry for adolescents.[12] Offering intergenerational collaborative opportunities for adolescents to grow, be creative, use their talents, and learn leadership skills with others is essential to establish the foundations of full, active, conscious, and participative adults in society or the church. Although it is important to remember that adolescents are still in the progress of self-discovery and their preferences, without the opportunity to learn, test, risk, and grow in the comfort of a family community or the church they will search elsewhere for acceptance and may find fulfillment of that desired sense of community in another group or belief system.

Dean's analysis of the NSYR data, through *Almost Christian*, started a necessary dialogue, and brought to the forefront the challenges that American adolescents have with spirituality, and their place within a contemporary religious context. Adolescents need the tools to become more community-minded in their lives, offering their talents not merely for their own benefit and good feelings, but for the betterment and love of others. To relate and build relationship with adolescents, adults in turn also need to be creative in their ability to change the cultural tide that is sweeping youth toward ennui regarding religious traditions and rituals. A full, active, conscious relationship with God needs to be the foundation of life in Christ. Without trust and abandon of their will to God's will, one is merely almost Christian.

Merton and the Authentic Self

Catholic youth ministry scholar Arthur Canales, as well as spiritual authors Richard Rohr and Joseph Martos, assert that self-discovery is an essential component associated with adolescence.[13] Brandy Quinn also echoed this nature of self-discovery in regard to adolescence, but utilized the phrase *purposeful explorer* to describe the drive within an adolescent to search for

12. See *Renewing the Vision*.

13. See Canales, *Noble Quest*; Rohr and Martos, *From Wild Man to Wise Man*.

their authenticity within and without of group ideology.[14] Thomas Merton's spirituality can be considered that of a perpetual seeker. His writings continually sought a deeper, more authentic, meaning of the self and relationship with God and community. Merton's writings are concerned with pursuing and living authentically, as God created; to live authentically for wholeness in body, mind, and spirit.

In *Seven Storey Mountain*, Merton recalled that although his father was Anglican and his mother was a Quaker, they did not practice their faith nor did they impose religious beliefs upon their children, allowing them to choose as they became older. From his earliest familial memories, Merton recalled that he was destined to live a life of authenticity and self-discovery: "Mother wanted me to be independent, and not to run with the herd. I was to be original, individual, I was to have a definite character and ideals of my own."[15] Already at a young age Merton recognized that his life was to be different than the norm, and to sustain such an identity in the world that attempts to conform people and ideas, great passion would be required.

Merton searched for authenticity through expansive exploration with Eastern spirituality, Communism, and philosophy, but was ultimately drawn to Catholicism, which he grew up having an aversion toward. An illustration of this deep-seeded prejudice of Catholicism was shown when Merton had purchased a book entitled *The Spirit of Medieval Philosophy*. His reaction to seeing an imprimatur, the Catholic statement of approval of a text, left him with a feeling of disgust and of being deceived.[16] The moment of purchasing and reading this text, along with researching and reading Gerard Manley Hopkins, created a new avenue of self-discovery in Merton that awoke a passionate desire toward Catholicism. In June 1938, when spiritually seeking guidance, Merton received the passionate advice from the famous and revered Hindu scholar, Mahanambrata Brahmachari, to read the

14. See: Quinn, "Purposeful Explorers."

15. Merton, *Seven Storey Mountain*, 12.

16. Merton, *Seven Storey Mountain*, 188.

spiritual texts Augustine's *Confessions* and Thomas a Kempis' *The Imitation of Christ* before seeking outside of his religious roots.[17]

"For me to be a saint means to be myself. Therefore, the problem of sanctity and salvation is in fact the problem of finding out who I am and of discovering my true self."[18] For Merton, holiness was not unattainable but very much a natural experience of becoming one's true self. Throughout his life, Merton offered an example of an individual striving for holiness and virtue by just being who he was through an authenticity founded in the courage to admit his own brokenness and failure, while not giving up hope.

As Merton wrote, and commented through his texts on spirituality, he continued to mature in understanding his place in the world through self-discovery, reflecting about this difference later in his life. One constant perspective that Merton held for authentic self-discovery was the nature of relationship with others. Merton stated that true freedom and authenticity of the self is only found in relationship with others:

> I do not find in myself the power to be happy merely by doing what I like. On the contrary, if I do nothing except what pleases my own fancy I will be miserable almost all of the time. This would never be so if my will had not been created to use its freedom in the life of others.[19]

Merton asserted that authentic self-discovery is found in relationship, not isolation, because human beings are naturally communal creatures and that the happiness of an individual is bound to the happiness of others.

Each individual Merton corresponded with felt like they encountered him personally, through his transparency and honesty. It is essential to remember that Merton communicated with countless individuals, as is well-documented through the collected volumes of his journals and letters. Throughout the context of those communications he demonstrated a consistent awareness and used purposeful language to that audience, political and/or cultural climate in which he was responding. It is easy to state that Merton's correspondence became an essential aspect of his vocation and ministry.[20]

17. See Croghan, "Mahanambrata Brahmachari and Thomas Merton," 3–10; Merton, *Seven Storey Mountain*, 216–17.

18. Merton, *New Seeds of Contemplation*, 31.

19. Merton, *No Man Is an Island*, 25.

20. See Merton, *Life in Letters*.

Media Examples for Adolescents

One of the challenges of distinguishing the true and false self with adolescents is that it can be easy for an adolescent to believe his, or her, true self is based only on feelings or emotion. Following these transient expressions can often leave an adolescent empty and isolated when the feeling does not turn out to be as great as the expectation. Adolescents are in need of tangible examples that discuss the deeper reality of the struggle between the true and false self.

The following examples from films can offer adolescents a conversation starter that can then bridge into a more complete discussion on authenticity. The following four examples have sparked deeper conversation and dialogue with adolescents about personal discernment and their vocation.

Fellowship of the Ring: The Lord of the Rings[21]

The 2001 Peter Jackson adaptation of J. R. R. Tolkien's epic story offers a direct example of vocation and discipleship which can be a challenging concept with adolescents. Many adolescents want to be seen as strong and independent leaders; they may also want to be identified as unique and apart from the crowd. How could a religious educator address discipleship amidst this trend in culture? The actions of the characters, terms, and symbolic nature of *the Lord of the Rings* offer an opportunity for adolescents a bridge to use for further theological inquiry.[22]

The characters of Frodo and Aragorn, as well as the excellent case study of the struggle between the persona and shadow through the choices and actions of Gollum throughout the series, offer adolescents characters, actions, and dialogue that can give voice to tangible struggles in their own lives that had not been examined previously by the adolescent. Here especially the concept of the ring of power called "my precious" can help adolescents identify those aspects of their lives where they have misplaced obsession for love or desire on something to a greater degree than God.

---

21. See Jackson, *Lord of the Rings*.

22. See Zoeller and Malewitz, "Tolkien's Allegory: Using Peter Jackson's Vision of Fellowship to Illuminate Male Adolescent Catholic Education," 66–83; and Jackson, *Lord of the Rings*.

The Dark Knight[23]

This 2008 action/adventure film follows the struggle between the comic hero, Batman, and the forces of chaos instigated by his nemesis, the Joker. Through this incarnation of the encounters of these characters, the Joker attempts to tempt Batman to break the only rule of his vocation as the just sentential of Gotham. Although there are several scenes that bring this struggle of identity, one particular visual brings this to a heated climax. While in an interrogation room, the Joker seems to push Batman to the brink of emotional stability and reason; through violent actions, the scene unfolds to Batman deciding between his true self, a defender of justice, and a false self of becoming the character the Joker was trying to mold him into.

Of Gods and Men[24]

This 2010 French drama follows the heroic spiritual virtue and transparent discernment of a community of Trappist monks in Algeria on the cusp of martyrdom. Although devoting their lives to help many of the poverty-stricken residents of the neighboring areas, the monks get caught in a struggle as a terrorist cell starts gaining control of the region during the Algerian Civil War. While watching this, adolescents can develop the opportunity to experience and discuss the extent that one would be willingly to go as a sacrificial witness of their authentic self.

Silence[25]

This 2016 dramatic Martin Scorsese film also offers an opportunity to challenge religious malaise by exploring the challenges of Jesuit Catholic missionaries during the purge of Christianity of seventeenth-century Japan. One of the most moving scenes of the film involves the trial and martyrdom of several faith-filled Japanese locals as their faith is tested through various means and, ultimately, because of their Christian faith, they are crucified in the ocean. As the scene unfolds many adolescents are challenged with what actions, rituals, and words mean in relation to the honesty of one's authentic self.

23. See Nolan, *Dark Knight*.
24. See Beauvois, *Of Gods and Men*.
25. See Scorsese, *Silence*.

To conclude this section on the authentic self and the maturity of Christianity during adolescence, I would like to turn to the wise insight offered by a spiritual director to the renowned author and mystic, Henri Nouwen:

> May all your expectations be frustrated. May all your plans be thwarted. May all of your desires be withered into nothingness, that you may experience the powerlessness and poverty of a child and sing and dance in the love of God the Father, the Son, and the Spirit.[26]

Practical Examen: Questions for Reflection

- Do *I* follow only those aspects of my life that are comfortable?
- Am *I* willing to take risks in my spiritual life for God to be more present in the world?
- Have *I* allowed adolescents to test, try, and discuss challenges and thoughts about their faith in a nonconfrontational environment?
- Do *I* honestly communicate, with adolescents, some of the faith struggles that I have experienced throughout my life?
- Do *I* take time to become familiar with contemporary films, television shows, or listen to music that could create a bridge with adolescents and faith?
- Am *I* honest with the need for continual journey and renewal to conform my life more to the call of Christ than my personal desires or the desires of culture?

---

26. Abegg, *Ragamuffin Prayers*, 43.

7

Passion

Zeal and Intimacy

A voice says in me—love: do trust love! Do not fear it, do not avoid it, do not take mere half-measures with it, but love, believe in it, without any special program.[1]

THOMAS MERTON WAS NOT a man devoid of passion, but lived it to the full. He embodied a life of passion throughout his advocacy, vocation, persistent exploration of philosophy and religion, and most clearly through his relationships. His journals especially illuminate a zealousness within his emotions and actions of the hermit-monk that can be eyebrow-raising to outsiders or initial Merton investigators. When approaching Merton's inner-most thoughts for the first time, it is easy to have the idea: this is not the person I thought he was. But is anyone really just who we think they are? It is easy to form impressions from momentary observations and assume that an individual is only what is projected and interpreted from an instance.

Merton's passion was not just exemplified through passing fancies within fits of anger or frustration with his superiors, or found in a mid-life love affair with M.,[2] but his passionate nature was present from his

1. Merton, *Journals of Thomas Merton*, 6:57.

2. Exploration of Merton's relationship with a nurse, M., throughout the summer of 1966 has been studied by many scholars. The extent of Merton and M.'s relationship is

earliest writings and continued through his thoughts and reflections from the Asian journals, at the conclusion of his life. Although Merton readers might focus on the passionate poetry and letters with M. as the height of Merton's passion, it is important to be aware that such passion was not hidden, closeted away until that moment, but was present in other aspects of his life. Suzanne Zuercher, reflected on Merton's thoughts on his relationship with M.'s best: "in that journal he revealed how vulnerable, how out of control, how wildly and immaturely romantic—and therefore how human—he could be."[3] Merton scholar, Michael W. Higgins also supports Merton's lifelong passion when he commented: "Throughout his life Merton was prone to extravagant responses, uncontainable enthusiasms, and occasionally intemperate judgments."[4]

Similarly, passion is a clear and recognized condition within the adolescent stage of life.[5] Thoughts and feelings are intense; they can fluctuate in extremes and are often difficult for adolescents to control, but nonetheless are passionate in response. Within the context of adolescent spirituality, passion could be described as intense desire, emotion, or excitement for an object, action, or relationship. The root of passion is difficult to address singularly but involves a complex interaction between hormones, peer relationships, hobbies, and the search for personal identity and preferences.

Adolescence: Passion or Lack of Control?

Examples of passionate expression of adolescents are often easily and clearly exhibited through athletics, the search for intimacy, and enthusiasm for various forms of leisure and entertainment. As a secondary educator, I particularly noticed this passionate drive within my adolescent students during the spring of 2018. Between February and March of that year, the students became obsessed with a particular game available on their iPads, instead of using their device for educational purposes at the school which implemented a one-to-one technological initiative. The game introduced

---

not a topic that will be deeply discussed here. It is only brought up as an example of one of the many examples of passion from the life of Merton. For further information, see Merton, *Journals of Thomas Merton*; Zuercher, *Ground of Love and Truth*; Forest, *Living with Wisdom*, 193–203; and Waldron, *Thomas Merton: The Exquisite Risk of Love*.

3. Zuercher, *Ground of Love and Truth*, 10.

4. Higgins, *Thomas Merton: Faithful Visionary*, 21.

5. Dean, *Almost Christian*.

for the iOS operating system was Fortnite, and with the release of Fortnite, the grades of the students dropped exponentially as many of them became addicted to the first-player multi-user shooter-survival game. Through 2018 and 2019 Fortnite became a cultural phenomenon, boasting more than 125 million players within a year of its initial release.[6] Although Fortnite is still rather popular over a year after its release on the iOS operating system, other online games have captured the zealous nature of the high school students, such as Madden Mobile.[7]

Such passion, in adolescents, does not just refer to obsession of video games but also encompasses the intensity of energy, vigor, and engagement of adolescents for academics, arts and drama, athletics, clubs, social media, as well as cultural rituals such as obtaining a driver's permit, Spring Break, and senior-year activities like prom, college visits, and moving away from their childhood home to live independently in a dorm, often for the first time. Beyond activities, one cannot miss the passion within adolescents and their desire for relationships. The biological drive of companionship, the desire of physical embrace, or, unfortunately, in the common practice of objection of the self or another for personal pleasure. The challenge that many adolescents face finds its basis on how to negotiate passionate feelings, face the consequences of actions driven by passion, and ultimately how to keep passion in balance. Adolescents eat, sleep, and live within a constant state of passion.

Time can also be a good measurement of one's passions; the more time devoted to an activity, the more one can become a living witness to that activity. There is an ancient liturgical saying, *lex orandi legem credendi constituit*, which can offer insight into the connectivity between time and passion. This phrase, loosely translated, states "the law of prayer constitutes the law of belief," or in an even more palatable form for adolescents, "how we pray shows what we believe." If prayer is understood for adolescents as order and time dedicated in relationship with God, this approach can bridge the language of sports, or other life activities, to the language of liturgy. Time, one of the most important currencies in life, can illuminate the importance of a ritual or activity in one's life. Based on the dedicated

---

6. See "Fortnite."

7. In fall 2019, using the battery function of the iOS system I found one particular high school senior who recorded 96 hours of Madden Mobile within a ten-day timeframe. Although that was the largest value I personally experienced many students were proud of their dedication to the game which became a game of comparison between peers as to who could exceed with the highest gaming percentage within a period of time.

amount of time to an activity, an adolescent can begin to quantify or qualify the various amounts of time devoted to sports, relationships, technology, and God.

Merton and a Life of Passion

From the perspective of an honest search for authenticity, Merton's writings realistically engage and relate to the struggles of the imperfect decisions and passions associated with adolescence. There are several moments throughout Merton's life when passion drives his actions. One of the first mentioned was chronicled about his perspective of the world after his father's death. In England with little guidance, an emancipated egoism developed in the adolescent Merton's mind and lifestyle.

> I concluded that I was now free of all authority, and that nobody could give me any advice that I had to listen to. Because advice was only the cloak of hypocrisy or weakness or vulgarity or fear. Authority was constituted by the old and the weak, and had its roots in their envy for the joys and pleasures of the young and strong.[8]

Thomas Merton engaged in passion toward all aspects of his life, his vocation, the depth of his knowledge, the furor of his writings, and his relationships with others. During his freshmen year at Clare College, Cambridge, Merton started experimenting and led a life full of passion, through excessive drinking and carousing. He also mentioned in *Seven Storey Mountain* the eye-opening and sexually freeing influence of reading Freud, Jung, and Adler.[9] Here Merton acknowledged that his appetites drove his actions, instead of being disciplined or controlling such appetites, which paralleled a contemporary emancipated stereotypical college student.

Another instance of passion exemplified by Merton was in the infancy of his conversion where he specifically recalled an experience, from February 1937, where he was captivated with a particular text sitting in the window at Scribner's bookshop in New York. After he purchased the book, *Spirit of Medieval Philosophy*, he became passionately frustrated that there was an imprimatur within the text, which indicated that the text was officially sanctioned by the Roman Catholic Church. At the time, Merton was

---

8. Merton, *Seven Storey Mountain*, 102

9. Merton, *Seven Storey Mountain*, 137.

disgusted and dismayed that the imprimatur of the book now connected the contents of the book with the church.

Merton later illustrated his passionate nature throughout his poetry, most especially through his collection of *Eighteen Poems*. The eighteen love poems are infused with passion, desire, and intensity that offer insight into the full force of nature that defined Merton's life.[10] Although not from the collection of the eighteen poems, the following poetic example clearly illustrates that Merton was a man that passionately exuded emotion through his poetry, even when discussing nature. This poem originally written by Merton in French still rings with power and passion through its English translation:

I BELIEVE IN LOVE

I believe in love
which sleeps and wakes up,
caught in the sperm of the seasons.

When I breathe my spring
on the fresh liturgical peaks of the hills
seeing all the trees and the green corn,
the anxious essence of my being
awakens with gaping yawns
and the adoration sounds like the legendary clocks
who ring their heavy chains in the womb of the ocean.

And when the looming sun of my summer
has stripped the gold flesh from my wheat
I find I have become rich: my song is pure,
this skeletal praise of Our Lady is my money.

O brothers, come with me.
Drink the wine of Melchisedech
while all the giant mountains
dressed in the vines of Isaias
sing peace.

Poems are born because love is like this
in the hollow heart of a man
and in the breast of my own broken rock.[11]

10. Waldron, *Thomas Merton: The Exquisite Risk of Love*.
11. Merton, "I Believe in Love," 825–26.

Throughout this example of his poetry, Merton clearly juxtaposes religious concepts with physical terms of passions and intimacy. Much like a spiritual mystic Merton's poetry exemplifies a passion and ecstasy present through nature and his religious experiences.

Merton also exhibited passion throughout other aspects of his life. Throughout several periods of acedia, restlessness, Merton planned to relocate from Gethsemani to other monasteries. In an examination of correspondences, Merton scholar Donald Grayston recounted that Merton passionately developed plans to move to a monastery in Camaldoli, Italy, in 1952;[12] ironically, this was the same location mentioned in *Seven Storey Mountain* that Merton was reading about when he experienced a deep vocational call to monastic life in 1941. In 1960, Merton again attempted to relocate to Cuernavaca, Mexico. Drawing on the journals of Merton, Roger Lipsey illustrated that in his thoughts Merton's desire to move was influenced in part by his passion regarding his preferences that challenged the views of his superior, James Fox:

> If I had to explain now to Dom James that I wanted to leave to go to Mexico—what on earth would I be able to say? I would be tongued tied. The things I could never say: I hate pontifical masses. I hate your idea of the liturgy—it seems to me to be a false, dead, repetition of words and gestures without spontaneity, without sincerity. You like to sing hymns because the melodies delight you. I can think of better ways with which to waste your time . . . I would say this and many other things, all adding up to one: our life here is too much of a lie. If that is really the case, then, since I can't do anything about it, I had better leave. But always the question remains: perhaps it is I who am the liar and perhaps leaving would be the greater lie.[13]

Merton's contempt for wasting time, his time and that of his abbot, comes full force here. Throughout his journals, passages like these indicate Merton vacillated with great turmoil on his decisions but was always remained passionate about his thoughts and actions. Like adolescents, there is a deep antagonistic tone toward control and a desire for independence.

---

12. See Grayston, *Thomas Merton and the Noonday Demon.*
13. Lipsey, *Make Peace Before the Sun Goes Down,* 122.

Merton's passion can also be noticed in his final journals during his Asian pilgrimage:

> I had my audience with the Dalai Lama this morning in his new quarters. It was a bright, sunny day—blue sky, the mountains absolutely clear . . . The Dalai Lama is most impressive as a person. He is strong and alert, bigger than I expected (for some reason I thought he would be small). A very solid, energetic, generous, and warm person, very capable of trying to handle enormous problems—none of which he mentioned directly.[14]

Merton's frank tone subtly displays his passion of meeting the revered spiritual leader. His use of the extreme adjectives, such as "most impressive," are phrases reserved in his vocabulary for individuals that have formed or monumentally change his life, such as Mark van Doren.[15] In his life and use of language, Thomas Merton was, in a truest sense of the term, an embodiment of passion. Much like a starstruck adolescent meeting their hero, Merton betrays an unbridled enthusiasm of meeting a learned and revered brother in spirituality.

14. Merton, *Asian Journals*, 100–101.
15. Merton, *Seven Storey Mountain*, 154.

Passion: Application with Adolescents

As Merton's faith evolved, from its infancy to one of great depths, he continued to read and learn from the heart of the great exemplars of faith. It is documented that Merton read biographies and modeled his prayer life based on the lives of passionate saints, such as Augustine, Bernard, John Vianney, and Thérèse of Lisieux. One way to help adolescents understand passion is through the similar example of individuals who lived passionate lives of virtue. Such exemplars of faith should be relatable, and their experiences be tangible to the life of an adolescent. But passion is not something that needs to be loud, abrasive, or forceful; it can be a mere witness of a force for change. The following are some examples of passionate men and women of virtue that have attracted the attention of adolescents throughout my theology courses throughout the years.

Elisabeth Leseur

Elisabeth Leseur's writings offer a fascinating insight into the culture and times of the anti-clerical secularization of France, during the 1800s. While reading Leseur's life and trials one is often struck by the earnest desire of Elisabeth to grow in her knowledge and practice of the faith. She was not satisfied with complacency in her education, and continued to read the writings of learned philosophers and theologians. Elisabeth's passion is a welcome reminder of the need to mature in knowledge and love to faithfully and authentically live the gospel.

One of the most eye-opening aspects of her life was the unwavering devotion of Elisabeth within her marriage even though her husband was a staunch atheist. The power of her interior life and strength through patience and fortitude offer a truly admirable witness to the pressure of ridicule.[16] Elisabeth's love was the mode of her evangelization. She never become hard-hearted, harsh, or condescending but always remained open and tireless to live the love of God to all of those around her.

There are many fascinating parallels between the lives of Thérèse of Lisieux and Elisabeth Leseur. Both women had a devoted interior life of prayer based on the writings of spiritual classics such as Thomas à Kempis and Francis deSales. They sought the conversion of hard-hearted atheists such as Henri Pranzini and Felix Leseur, often feeling great amounts of

---

16. See Leseur, *My Spirit Rejoices*; and Leseur, *Selected Writings*.

isolation in their respective communal lives, and enduring suffering toward the end of their lives, through the illnesses of tuberculosis and cancer, respectively, but ultimately living in love and joy in the midst of their trials.

John Paul II

Pope John Paul II's homily in Victory Square in 1979, offered the power of hope to a nation of citizens that were beaten into docility by the power of the Polish communist government. Since World War II, many Catholic leaders like Archbishop Stepinc of Croatia, Cardinal Mindszenty of Hungary, and Cardinal Wyszynski of Poland were martyred or jailed because of their faith; which put great fear in the mindset of the faithful about religion in the public eye. The propaganda of communist Eastern Europe and Russia tried to indoctrinate the younger generation to the danger of religion by limiting the people to one vision of the world. Although citizens tried to create a voice through their actions, such as the act of self-immolation of Ryszard Siwiec in 1968, the government and media were able to distort his message against the government to a mental illness.

In 1979, John Paul II's celebration of the nine-hundredth anniversary of the martyrdom of Saint Stanislaus, a previous bishop of Krakow who died challenging the corrupt Polish king of 1079, thwarted such propaganda plans of the communist government.[17] The Pontiff's words resounded the inextricable identity of Christianity and the history of Poland. Through the mentioning of national symbols such as the Tomb of the Unknown Soldier, to renew the conscious of liberty and freedom from Polish history John Paul II reminded the Polish people of their rights and freedom through their own history. John Paul II's words carried a raw and authentic power because of his national identity and struggled experiences with the Polish people through communist oppression.

Francis Xavier Nguyen Van Thuan

The life and struggles of Archbishop Francis Xavier Nguyen Van Thuan offer an example of a humble individual who, though in imprisonment and exile, was able to still find joy and passion through even the most challenging of circumstances. On April 24, 1975, Van Thuan was assigned as the

17. See Weigel, *Witness to Hope.*

archbishop of Saigon and six days later, when Saigon fell, he was captured by the communist government and held as a prisoner in a reeducation camp for thirteen years, nine of which were in solitary confinement. Throughout his incarceration he was able to write and smuggle small words of hope for his community outside of the prison walls. The collection of his passionate plea of hope and joy in the midst of his people's suffering was collected together in a manuscript called *The Road of Hope*.[18] Van Thuan exemplifies the life of an individual who can love through suffering, find joy in life, and spread faith through small acts of kindness.

Practical Examen: Questions for Reflection

- Do *I* show enthusiasm when an adolescent may share something that they are passionate about with me?

- Do *I* ever invite an adolescent to share in one of my passions, within the community or church, so that they might learn that adulthood includes joyful and life meaning experiences?

- Am *I* afraid to share difficult news or circumstances with an adolescent or child because I do not want to burden them with adult issues?

- Do *I* witness joy when participating in ministry, with the Church or going to praise God at Mass or Church services?

- Am *I* willing to share small appropriate signs of affection with my spouse as a witness of continued passion and unity for children and young adults of the family to recognize that the relationship is grounded in love within the marriage?

- Do *I* only exhibit passion for entertainment activities, such as sports, video games, or those things that make me feel good? Are *my* actions a witness of saying only those things have meaning and bring joy to my life?

---

18. See Van Thuan, *Road of Hope*; and Van Thuan, *Fives Loaves & Two Fish*.

8

Athletics

Sports and Personal Discipline

Souls are like athletes, that need opportunity worthy of them, if they are to be tried and extended and pushed to their full use of their powers, and rewarded according to their capacity.[1]

ALTHOUGH THERE HAVE BEEN many comparisons between the intense and rigorous training of athletes and spiritual development, Thomas Merton's quote above offers a direct and spiritual allegory for reflection. This quotation, from *The Seven Storey Mountain*, contextually occurred as Merton reflected upon his father's battle with cancer. This metaphor offered a purposeful reminder for the reader, as well as Merton, that the fights and battles of others are not always evident through the physical senses alone. Reflecting on that incident from his life Merton did not realize until later the depths of his father's capacity to be refined through the spirit, as it was mentioned in *The Seven Storey Mountain* that he thought his father had finished the struggle and was giving up, but to the amazement of Merton his father continued to fight the illness.[2]

Individuals of ordinary athletic skill sets often appreciate the excitement and enthusiasm that is present in a victorious underdog story,

1. Merton, *Seven Storey Mountain*, 92.
2. Merton, *Seven Storey Mountain*, 92.

especially when related to sports. The story of the victory of an underdog often offers a sense of possibility to everyone that the impossible could potentially occur. Through films such as the *Rocky* series, *Rudy*, and *The Miracle* Hollywood has presented stories of the underdog, who through grit and determination can find resurrection from the gravest of circumstances. True enough, this message parallels the Christian story of resurrection but what can adolescents interpret and learn from when watching an athletic film or underdog story used an analogy, within a sports context?

Adolescence and Athletics

Athletics have become a rite of passage for most adolescents. From a young age, youth learn how to celebrate and mourn through collective experiences on a court, field, or rink. Popular American television shows, in the recent decades, specifically geared for an adolescent audience have included a central plot that revolves around athletics, such as *One Tree Hill* (2003–12), *Friday Night Lights* (2006–11), and *Ballers* (2015–19). ESPN has also capitalized on this demand in viewer attention through their production of documentaries of the extraordinary feats of athletes and sporting events within the *30-for-30* series (2009–present).

Many adolescents view professional athletes as role models and idols within their perspective sports. Much of this athletic heroism is not a new phenomenon but can be illustrated in adolescents across previous generations and cultures. From rugby and soccer in the European and African continents as well as South America to baseball, basketball, and football in North American sports, athleticism communicates deep truths of the human experience to individuals and communities.

As an aside, as a high school teacher I have experienced that one of the most popular genre choices by male adolescents for the annual summer reading book selection is biography, particularly of an athlete or a highly respected coach. Without digressing too much into history, only two generations ago many adolescents found inspiration through athletes like: Joe DiMaggio, Jackie Robinson, Muhammad Ali, Gordie Howe, and Wilt Chamberlain. About a generation-and-a-half ago athletes such as Hank Aaron, Walter Payton, and Kareem Abdul Jabbar, and later Fernando Valenzuela, Bo Jackson, Michael Jordan, and Wayne Gretzky caught the attention of youth. More recently athletes like LeBron James, Miguel Cabrera, and Tom Brady fill such spots of sports idols. The tragedy of the death of basketball star Kobe Bryant exemplified the role that athletes have within the local community and nation, as there was a pallor and collective mourning of the loss of such an athlete through celebrations that transcended the sport of basketball.[3] No matter the player, team, or nationality sports transcend racial stereotypes and artificial societal boundaries.

Sports: A Game or a Religion?

> In order to attract young people who are only marginally engaged in the life of the Church or not engaged at all, it is necessary that those who catechize adopt a missionary attitude. This implies a willingness to go out to where young people can be found.[4]

This section may be quite polarizing for some readers, but like Merton, it is important to examine the world in which we live. For many adolescents, athletics have come to fill a void left in the wake of a post-Christian society; where else does one encounter rituals, the honoring of heroes, clear-cut rules, and the enforcement of said rules? Since the mid-1900s, the American pasttime of baseball had captured a generation of youth. Baseball cards were collected, compared, and stats were analyzed. Records were set and become canon—it was so essential that the canon would not change that when Roger Maris surpassed Babe Ruth for the record of number of home runs in a season it had to be designated with an "*" to indicate that Maris needed more games to surpass the record, since the 1961 season included more games than when Ruth originally set the record. Likewise, athletes who break the rules are held to dire consequences such as Pete Rose and his inability to be considered as a member of the Baseball Hall of Fame in Cooperstown, New York, or scathing criticism of steroid use or sign-stealing. The purity and sacredness of the game needs to be preserved.

Athletics: Finding Meaning in Discipline and Wholeness

Today, youth are finding meaning by playing multiple sports and by multiple rules. What is obvious, though, is that sports rule the lives of adolescents. It is through athleticism that an adolescent can feel and be full of zeal, passion,

3. See Gan and Jozuka, "Chinese Fans in Mourning."
4. *Joy of Adolescent Catechesis*, §12.

heroism, and receive accolades. Athletic seasons are no longer restricted to a few months out of the year but have evolved into a year-long experience of conditioning, strategic preparation, and training. Colleges and universities award large monetary scholarships for athletes, and as prompted throughout the sports world, athletes that can make it to the professional level usually find wealth, pleasure, and popularity as a prize. But what happens when such dreams are dashed, and come crashing down?

There was no better expression of this confusion and anxiety than a poem entitled "I Can't Read" delivered by Lamont Carey on HBO's *Def Poetry Jam* from 2007.[5] The poem offers an image of a student that is valued only for his athletic abilities; who seemingly is passed from grade to grade and is able to cover up the fact that he does not know how to read through humor and athletics. At the conclusion of the poem Carey questioned: when the athletic ability is gone, what is there to do when *I* still can't read? Merton offered a parallel analogy on the challenge of this aspect of sports, if it was just viewed from the stance of winning and material success:

> The score is not what matters. Life does not have to be regarded as a game in which scores are kept and somebody wins. If you're too intent on winning, you will never enjoy playing. If you are too obsessed with success, your life will probably be wasted.[6]

The growth and maturation of both the spiritual and the physical body is an essential part of the development of the whole human person. Contemporary society often recognizes the need for attention to the development of the physical and encourages adolescents to be involved in sports and teams to develop individual skills, but also to develop skills of group building and community interaction. There are countless stories that explore the way athletics have offered the opportunity to better the life of individuals searching for a way out of their particular life circumstances.[7] Some authors, though, have now started challenging this traditional perspective of sports as the monetary savior but view it more as a dangerous gamble. In 2008, Director of the Aspen Institute Sports and Society Program Tom Farrey penned *Game On*, which challenged traditional stereotypes of the focus on competition and individual achievement in athletics. Following Farrey's analysis was Mark Hyman, journalist and professor, who

5. See Carey, *Def Poetry Jam*.

6. Merton, "Learning to Live," 12.

7. See Bidini, *Home and Away*.

wrote *Until It Hurts* as well as coauthored *Concussions and Our Kids*, which explored the growing amount of athletic injuries plaguing youth, that can leave consequences for the remainder of their life.

Sports and the Tradition of the Church

Although most student-athletes are painfully aware that they will not receive college scholarships or become a professional athlete countless adolescents still put the effort, pain, and suffering into the sport for the opportunity for such prestige. There is a great draw in athletics to find a true sense of community; a team. The concept of community has been at the heart of the Christian mission since its beginning. Paul of Tarsus discussed the concept of community through the analogy of the body of Christ, the community of the faithful (1 Cor 12:12–27). Here this image serves as an important parallel. If adolescents desire more to be part of a community or team, what is missing from the church today that does not offer that sense of deep and longing community within the body of Christ?

> Do you not know that in a race the runners all compete, but only one receives the prize? Run in such a way that you may win it. Athletes exercise self-control in all things; they do it to receive a perishable wreath, but we an imperishable one. (1 Cor 9:24–25)

Beyond the use of sport metaphors throughout the letters of Paul of Tarsus, many other saints and theologians have utilized sports and athletics as a tangible comparison to the Christian witness. A recent athletic theologian who could be an exemplar for adolescents is the witness of the life of John Paul II, who had more than thirty addresses directly focused on the importance of sports and their connection with spirituality.

> Playing sports has become very important today, since it can encourage young people to develop important values such as loyalty, perseverance, friendship, sharing and solidarity. Precisely for this reason, in recent years it has continued to grow even more as one of the characteristic phenomena of the modern era, almost a "sign of the times" capable of interpreting humanity's new needs and new expectations. Sports have spread to every corner of the world, transcending differences between cultures and nations. Because of the global dimensions this activity has assumed, those involved in sports throughout the world have a great responsibility. They are called to make sports an opportunity for meeting and dialogue,

over and above every barrier of language, race or culture. Sports, in fact, can make an effective contribution to peaceful understanding between peoples and to establishing the new civilization of love.[8]

Although he discussed athletics frequently John Paul II was also an avid sportsman in his youth, known for skiing and kayaking.[9] During an interview, in 1997, when his physical abilities were starting to deteriorate, he confessed to the biographer George Weigel: "I used to be a sportsman, you know."[10]

Like other holy people throughout the history of the church talented athletes were inspired to adopt their physical discipline into a spiritual dimension, such as the Jesuit cofounder Francis Xavier, who was long-jump and high-jump champion at the University of Paris in the 1500s.[11] A more contemporary example would be Pier Giorgio Frassati, patron of young Catholics, youth groups, and World Youth Day. Frassati, an avid mountain climber, swimmer, and bicyclist drew on his athleticism as inspiration for a disciplined spiritual life.[12] As John Paul II stated during Frassati's Beatification Homily:

> His love for beauty and art, his passion for sports and mountains, his attention to society's problems did not inhibit his constant relationship with the Absolute. Entirely immersed in the mystery of God and totally dedicated to the constant service of his neighbor: thus we can sum up his earthly life![13]

Merton: On Athletics

Thomas Merton, although not a stellar athlete himself, appreciated the importance of physical development for the wholeness of the human person. This type of discipline should not be the only aspect of human formation but, as Merton acknowledged, parallels the development and sustained formation for the spirit, as well. Athletics cannot be reduced to conditioning for a game but to be successful also depends on awareness of the necessity

8. John Paul II, "Jubilee of Sports People, October 29, 2000," §2.

9. Weigel, *Witness to Hope*, 116, 761.

10. Weigel, *Witness to Hope*, 1634.

11. Zipple, *Xavier: Missionary and Saint*.

12. Michaels, *Saints for Our Times*, 101.

13. John Paul II, "Beatification Homily," §4.

of full, active, conscious participation needed to stay focused and engaged in the action and embodiment of the sport or activity, as is reminded in the Constitution on the Sacred Liturgy from the Second Vatican Council.[14]

> Actually "mortification of the flesh" is comparable to training for athletics: and no more harmful if it is done the way we are meant to do it: we eat only what we need, the barest essentials . . . we do things that are a little painful and tiring. What is there about this that is different from the life of a poor laborer? Or of an athlete in training?[15]

Thomas Merton was well aware of the excitement of sports and used sports analogies in his teachings and writings to help illustrate engaging life and its importance.[16] In *Seven Storey Mountain*, Merton recounts that while he was at Clare College and Columbia University, he had experience as an athlete, involved with rowing and cross-country. Although Merton lived the life of sports, pleasure, and passion, during that time he plainly admitted he did not make a very good athlete.[17] Later in his life Merton reminisced about his youthful athletic physique compared to the ailments of his aging body:

> And there I am: it shakes me! I am the young rugby player, the lad from Cambridge, vigorous, light, vain, alive, obviously making a joke of some sort. The thing that shakes me: I can see that that was a different body from the one I have now—one entirely young and healthy, one that did not know sickness, weakness, anguish, tension, fatigue.[18]

Although not the image referred to in the previous quotation, the following photo which includes an adolescent Thomas Merton illustrates a sense of his athletic youth, as previously described. Here Merton stands stern, focused, and determined with his Oakham rugby team, much like contemporary adolescents would pose with fierce athleticism.[19]

14. Paul VI, "Sacrosanctum Concilium," §14.

15. Merton, *Journals of Thomas Merton*, 1:138.

16. Rembert, "Merton on Sports and Spirituality," 18–25.

17. Merton, *Seven Storey Mountain*, 134, 166, 173, 178.

18. Merton, *Journals of Thomas Merton*, 5:325.

19. In the following photo, Thomas Merton is located the third from the left, in the back row of students.

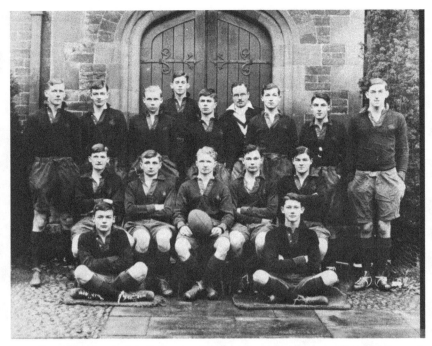

Ron Rembert, Professor and Merton enthusiast, explored Merton's use of sports metaphors throughout his conferences offered for the novices at Gethsemani. In his article, "Merton on Sports and Spirituality," Rembert reflected that Merton specifically drew parallels to football and boxing in several lectures.[20] It seems that Merton gained an interest in the discipline and routine of the demand upon the football athletes at Bonaventure College. Merton expressed his respect and affection of their study habits, dedication, and insight into human behavior in *Seven Storey Mountain*.[21]

Athletics: Application with Adolescents

Many adolescents are familiar with the trials and grueling schedules of organized sports, but the question remains: what do they learn from it? As a high school teacher, I have noticed adolescents fasting to cut weight for a particular class in wrestling, I have noticed students consuming energy drinks to stay awake during practice and late games, and I have also experienced adolescents who have been so injured that they can no longer play

20. See Rembert, "Merton on Sports and Spirituality."

21. Merton, *Seven Storey Mountain*, 335.

the sport that they love again. The concepts of sacrifice, fasting, and follow-ing natural rhythms of the body can be doorways to assist adolescents into a deeper understanding of their athletic experiences.

As mentioned previously there are countless films and documentaries that can assist adolescents in gaining a greater appreciation between the connection of athletics and spirituality, about themes on community, dis-cipline, fortitude, endurance, and resurrection from failure. The following examples have engaged students to reassess and explore the present situa-tions of their lives within a spiritual context.

"The 16th Man"[22]

Nelson Mandela was a controversial political resistor and revolutionary. His struggle and work for reconciliation for a South African population divided by apartheid has been compared by some scholars to the social justice work of Ghandi and Martin Luther King Jr. Although Mandela utilized violent measures early in his life, through his twenty-seven–year incarceration, Mandela changed his approach to nonviolent dialogue after his release in 1990. He later became the president of South Africa from 1994 to 1999. For the remainder of his life Mandela continued to work to establish reconcili-ation throughout the country.

One of Nelson Mandela's most strategic examples of aligning the interests of South Africans after apartheid was through sports. As chron-icled through the 2009 film *Invictus,* and *ESPN's* "The 16th Man," Nelson Mandela used the country's obsession for rugby to unify the population together. Instead of removing or changing the symbol of the National rugby team of South Africa, the Springbok, which was interpreted by many South Africans as a racist symbol of apartheid control, Mandela argued that the symbol needed to stay but that its meaning needed to be changed. Mandela argued that true unity could never be found by destroying or villainizing the past but in actions that signified a new all-inclusive era of South Africa:

> Sport has the power to change the world. It has the power to in-spire, it has the power to unite people in a way that little else does. It speaks to youth in a language they understand. Sport can create hope, where once there was only despair. It is more powerful than

22. See Bestall, "16th Man."

governments in breaking down racial barriers. It laughs in the face of all types of discrimination.[23]

"Into the Wind"[24]

This 2010 *ESPN 30 for 30* documentary focuses on the life of the Canadian cancer advocate Terry Fox. In 1980, when he was in his early twenties and his cancer was in remission, but with one leg amputated, Fox decided to raise awareness of cancer victims by running across Canada, from the East Coast to the West. Throughout the journey he met other younger sufferers from the disease, who looked up to Fox and his witness. Fox needed to stop 143 days into his trek due to the return of the illness; he later succumbed to the disease but a Marathon of Hope has endured in his memory as a lasting testament to the lengths of an ordinary citizen to change and unify the hope and advocacy of a nation.

"You Don't Know Bo"[25]

This ESPN *30 for 30* documentary, from 2012, progresses through the athletic career of Vincent "Bo" Jackson. Rising from stardom in high school and collegiate sports, Bo became a major league athlete in two sports: baseball and football. He currently is the only person to be elected an All-Star in both the MLB and NFL. After a career-ending hip injury in 1991, Bo had to endure intensive physical rehabilitation but was eventually able to return to play major league baseball. He retired from professional baseball in 1994, but the wonders and astounding stories of his athletic achievements are still discussed and marveled. Through the witness and testimony of coaches, players, and Bo himself, adolescents can experience the feats of an amazing athlete but also understand the power and ritual of generations of storytelling. Throughout the documentary Bo acknowledges that the talents were given to him by God. He also stressed the importance of using those talents and persevering when life dramatically changes purpose and meaning.

---

23. Mandela, "Inaugural Laureus Lifetime Achievement Award," para. 1.
24. See Nash, "Into the Wind."
25. See Bonfiglio, "You Don't Know Bo."

"Brave in the Attempt"[26]

In 2015, the ESPN series *30 for 30* released a documentary on the advocating work of Eunice Kennedy Shriver and her development of the special Olympics for youth and young adults with disabilities. Shriver, inspired by the challenges that her sister Rose Mary Kennedy faced, originally opened up the Shriver family home and estate as a summer camp for youth with disabilities. As the vision of the camp grew, Shriver had the vision for a national experience that gave youth with disabilities the opportunity to experience sports and competition that paralleled the experience of other athletes. The first Special Olympics was held in Chicago in 1968, and the institution has been expanding ever since. The once-backyard summer camp evolved into an international celebration, and gave witness to the dignity of all human beings, especially in countries that had often hidden or ostracized individuals that with disabilities.

"The '85 Bears"[27]

The 2016 documentary, from the ESPN *30 for 30 series*, "The '85 Bears" focuses on relationships between the players from the championship season and their defensive coach, Buddy Ryan. Switching from the present day to highlights of the development of the championship team, the documentary builds anticipation of the athletic feats of the players in their prime, but takes time to examine the importance of lifelong relationships and the effects individuals have throughout one's life. It offers a powerful reminder of the struggle and courage of deteriorating health and the desire for authentic community.

Practical Examen: Questions for Reflection

- Do *I* celebrate the passion and excitement that adolescents and youth have for the joy in sports, through positive sports and encouragement?
- Have *I* contributed to the culture of athletic aggression or pressured youth/adolescents to play or continue a sport?

---

26. See Mitchell, "Brave in the Attempt."
27. See Hehir, "'85 Bears."

- Do *I* share undistracted time and experiences with youth or adolescents at a sporting event or activity?

- Have *I* explored Thomas Merton's analogy of the discipline of athletics as a perspective for my spiritual growth and development?

- Do *I* neglect to spend time watching family members' athletic games?

- Have *I* volunteered to help a youth or adolescent learn a new sporting activity?

9

The Arts, Part I—Music/Poetry

The Appreciation of Creative Expression

Happiness is not a matter of intensity but of balance and order and rhythm and harmony.[1]

THOMAS MERTON WAS MUCH more complex and creative than a manufactured bestselling celebrated spiritual author. His words continue to resonate an authentic, passionate advocacy for the dignity of all of humanity. Merton was an individual who could not be labeled, or placed inside of a box.[2] He had a constant desire of expanding, learning, and engaging the world which developed into a multitude of interests beyond the walls of a Midwestern American monastery and into the milieu of the secular twentieth-century American consciousness. He was a poet, a voracious reader, an artist, a man of meditation, a bridge of interreligious dialogue and discussion, and a voluminous correspondent.[3]

1. Merton, *No Man Is an Island*, 127.

2. Atkinson, *Many Stories and Last Days of Thomas Merton.*

3. See Merton, *Collected Poems of Thomas Merton*; Lipsey, *Angelic Mistakes*; Hall, *Day of a Stranger.*

Adolescents: Music and the Arts

Adolescents find meaning and happiness through the arts, especially music and lyrical poetry. Choir, musicals, band, and clubs that help students develop skills on instruments like guitar, percussion, and jazz music are mainstays in high school environments. Adolescents seek out communities to be a part of and contribute to; many young people who are musicians have found appreciation through starting bands with friends or neighbors.

In contemporary culture, many adolescents share their music talents through online venues, such as YouTube. Some of these musical contributors hope to become a new discovered and viral sensation like other musicians who originally were founded from the same internet venue, such as Justin Bieber, Carly Rae Jepsen, and Ed Sheeran. This type of imitation of online musical success has its ups and downs, though, as demonstrated through the infamous song and music video "Friday" by Rebecca Black, who at fourteen became a viral star but through jest and ridicule.[4] With the heights of viral stardom so high, it is challenging for adolescents to understand and negotiate the such extreme reactions to their dreams.

Music has become part of the DNA of our culture. Instead of just having one or two musicians who become the voice for a generation, adolescents thrive on a consistent connection to playlists that can cycle through their favorite musicians and songs, as well as similar artists, through applications like Spotify and Apple Music.

Understanding the Arts: Music and Poetry through a Scriptural Context

Music and poetry also serve as the fabric of Scripture. The Hebrew Scriptures include one hundred fifty psalms, prayer-songs, of various tone for praise and deeper emotion connection and relationship with God. As one of the first examples of sung prayer, Moses and Miriam led the Israelites in songs of praise of YHWH's victory over the Egyptian army at the Red Sea (Exod 15). The Christian Scriptures are also full of worship that incorporates the singing of hymns and psalms since its infancy (Eph 5:19), sung prayer (1 Cor 11:4–5), vocal thanksgiving (Eph 5:20; Heb 13:15), and instruction (1 Cor 14:26; Col 3:16). The Gospel of Luke (the Canticles of

---

4. Trepany, "Rebecca Black Opens Up about Depression, Bullying She Faced for Viral Video 'Friday.'"

Mary and Zachariah) and the Prologue of the Gospel of John (John 1:1–18) preserve hymns that were likely used in the worship within the early church.

Scripture clearly indicates that Jesus and his apostles sang together while they prayed together: "When they had sung the hymn, they went out to the Mount of Olives" (Matt 26:30). Musical prayer and the rhythm of song has lifted the spirits throughout the ages.

> The power of sacred music increases the honor given to God by the Church in union with Christ, its Head. Sacred music likewise helps to increase the fruits which the faithful, moved by the sacred harmonies, derive from the holy liturgy. These fruits, as daily experience and many ancient and modern literary sources show, manifest themselves in a life and conduct worthy of a Christian.[5]

Not only lifting the spirit, music can also help bridge God and humanity through cultural expression. Recognizing the scared connection between, music, culture, and the human expression is essential in ministry today. As the Constitution on the Liturgy from the Second Vatican Council states:

> In certain parts of the world, especially mission lands, there are peoples who have their own musical traditions, and these play a great part in their religious and social life. For this reason due importance is to be attached to their music, and a suitable place is to be given to it, not only in forming their attitude toward religion, but also in adapting worship to their native genius.[6]

Merton and Rhythm: Music and Poetry

Thomas Merton was moved by music. He loved jazz and was fascinated with the folk musicians of the 1960s, especially Bob Dylan. Merton mentioned that he specifically enjoyed "Obviously 5 Believers" from *Blonde on Blonde* in correspondence to Suzanne Butorovich, his adolescent friend and pen pal in California.[7] The folk singer-songwriter and social activist Joan Baez and a friend visited Merton at Gethsemani in 1967. She recalled, "After we had our picnic in the field, we came back to his hermitage. He pulled out a bottle of Scotch and began to drink, and we talked for about nineteen

---

5. Pius XII, "Musicae Sacrae," §32.

6. Paul VI, "Sacrosanctum Concilium," §119.

7. Merton, "Letter to Suzanne Butorovich, June 22, 1967," 309.

hours."[8] One can image what Merton would discuss with Baez during this time. Nonetheless, Merton felt the passion of music move him into the point of becoming one with the rhythm of the tune. In her documentary film *Day of the Stranger*, Cassidy Hall brilliantly illustrates this through a scene where Merton is becoming in tune with a particular jazz album. As the music is playing, this jazz odyssey enfolds as Merton starts dialoguing in short bursts and exclamations with the music from the album, much like a deep connection within gospel communities, where the congregation becomes one with the music, feeling, and spiritual connection of the divine moment.

> Let us obey life, and the Spirit of Life that calls us to be poets, and we shall harvest many new fruits for which the world hungers—fruits of hope that have never been seen before . . . Come, dervishes: here is the water of life. Dance in it.[9]

Merton: On Music

Merton was not a stereotypical contemplative monk and made that clearly known throughout his writings. Since his youth Merton was fond of jazz music, and was a musician who had rhythm to play piano and bongos well.[10] He was taken with the folk music scene of the early 1960s, particularly enjoying the lyrics and music of Bob Dylan and The Beatles. Much of Merton's correspondence with adolescents includes some connection to the topic of music. This is especially demonstrated with Suzanne Butorovich. Throughout these letters she discussed her love of the Beatles with Merton, who also mentioned that he enjoyed *Revolver*, and after receiving a copy of handwritten lyrics from the Sgt. Pepper album from Suzanne, confided that he had an agent on his behalf who was supposed to sneak him a copy of the album.[11] Throughout these letters Suzanne also discussed other popular musicians from 1967 and 1968, like Jefferson Airplane. Merton was clearly fascinated with pop culture, like the Beatles, and how the messages of such poets and entertainers connected to God and theology.[12]

8. Baez, "Joan Baez," 42.

9. Merton, "Message to Poets," 160–61.

10. Richard Sisto, personal communication, August 2, 2017.

11. Merton, "Letter to Suzanne Butorovich, July 18, 1967," 310.

12. In an aside, Merton wrote a response to *The New Yorker*, regarding a piece from

Merton: On Poetry

Thomas Merton was not just fascinated with song and tunes but used words to express deep and penetrating meanings through poetic verse. But the use of his words were not just for entertainment purposes, Merton was moved for a purpose; these poems were words of advocacy and challenge. Merton's were full of a powerful presence of voice from beyond the walls of a monastery trying to help a world disconnected from authentic reality. The following examples

of Merton's poetry are to offer a taste of his use of language to elicit emotion and conversion, of heart and action.

HAGIA SOPHIA (excerpt)

1. *Dawn. The Hour of Lauds.*

There is in all visible things an invisible fecundity, a dimmed light, a meek namelessness, a hidden wholeness. This mysterious Unity and Integrity is Wisdom, the Mother of all, *Natura naturans*. There is in all things an inexhaustible sweetness and purity, a silence that is found of action and joy . . . This is at once my own being, my own nature, and the Gift of my Creator's Thought and Art within me, speaking as Hagia Sophia, speaking as my sister, Wisdom.[13]

In this brief excerpt of "Hagia Sophia," Merton realigns the focus of the reader from a dull apathic connection with traditional religious concepts to an engaging and lively expression of faith embodiment in the totality of real life; one's own being. Humanity is bound in a divine mystery

---

August 27, 1966, that moved him to tears because of its theological significance for him. The article revolved around John Lennon and the Beatles' fame and their comment about their popularity compared to Jesus, at the time. Merton, *Road to Joy*, 343.

13. Merton, "Hagia Sophia," 363.

of known and unknown as it seeks wisdom from God to find its ultimate purpose, happiness.

ORIGINAL CHILD BOMB (excerpts: ll. 32, 33, 40, and 41)

32: The bomb exploded within 100 feet of the aiming point. The fireball was 18,000 feet across. The temperature at the center of the fireball was 100,000,000 degrees. The people who were near the center became nothing. The whole city was blown to bits and the ruins all caught fire instantly everywhere, burning briskly. 70,000 people were killed right away or died within a few hours. Those who did do not die at once suffered great pain. Few of them were soldiers.

33: The men in the plane perceived that the raid had been successful, but they thought of the people in the city and they were not perfectly happy. Some felt they had done wrong. But in any case they had obeyed orders. "It was war."

40: As to the Original Child that was now born, President Truman summed up the philosophy of the situation in a few words. "We found the bomb" he said "and we used it."

41: Since that summer many other bombs have been "found." What is going to happen? At the time of writing, after a season of brisk speculation, men seem to be fatigued by the whole question.[14]

In these brief sections of "Original Child Bomb," Merton offered a no-holds-barred approach to the devastation and trivialization of war. Using facts about the atomic bomb, Merton shows how much our own language betrays our apathic attitude toward the value of human life and the lack of respect for the power of destruction that humanity now yields, or gave birth to. Merton's poems are a needed reminder of the need to wake up to the rhythms that define our realities.

Rhythm: Through the Words and Experiences of Adolescents

To have adolescents experience the theme of rhythm, through a tangible medium, I created the opportunity for the students to experience and dialogue about being part of a drum circle, which was the closest nod I could think of to Merton's enjoyment of playing bongos. The adolescents later reflected on the musical experience through their personal journals. The

---

14. Merton, "Original Child Bomb," 300–302.

purpose of this reflection activity was to create an opportunity to invite the students to reflect and share about their experiences and the nature of collaboration.

The following narrative vignettes serve as supporting evidence of aesthetic engagement by demonstrating sensory, logical, emotional, and ethical connections expressed by the students throughout the course of the implementation.

To help the students initially experience the need for awareness and collaboration in music the exploratory curriculum included a couple music videos of the viral sensation band *Walk Off the Earth*. The following responses were from collected student reflections after watching the music videos:

> Larry [written response]: They would stop and look around at their partners every once in a while to gain a perspective of when they should play . . . They would listen to each others' playing to stabilize themselves.

> Scotty [written response]: They kept on looking at each other & each of them moved their bodies the way the song went to keep in rhythm . . . They would nod their heads to keep rhythm & once they would look at each other's guitar & hands to make sure they were in rhythm.

> Jerome [written response]: The musicians were constantly looking and watching each other in order to adjust or continue the rhythm.

> Eric [written response]: They listen to the rhythm and know the timing of when to come in or do their part . . . They watched the other, if one stopped then joined back in.

> Oakland [written response]: They would look at each other and see what they were doing. They would also listen to the sounds the others were making . . . They would move their bodies in certain ways to keep up the beat and rhythm.

Through these responses, the students were interpreting that there is important communication that can occur between others beyond the use of verbal language. One student specifically recognized that individuals can adjust their behavior by listening to and watching others, from the context of the musicians in the music videos. Similar to the group activity on the session of order, the adolescents again interpreted that each person in the group offers a unique part that completes the whole.

After their initial thoughts and experiences, the students were also invited to journal about their personal experiences of the drum circle. The student-participant responses in the journals further explained and explored their personal experiences and interpretations of the activities as well as expanding the context beyond the activities to other situations such as personal relationships and society at-large:[15]

> Harold [written response]: The drum circle was fully dependent on rhythm . . . Everyone had a part to play in the song and this was one of the first experiences I had where I look at St. Peter Faber [School] as a community . . . everyone is dependent on one another, and to me that is the definition of community.

> Richard [written response]: The drum circle and the clips we watched today show me that everyone has a role in society and that we all must work together to maintain rhythm.

> Steve [written response]: In the experience of drumming I learned a few things . . . If people focus on the rhythm of life the community will be successful in many cases.

> Larry [written response]: When we participated in the drum circle, we were told to listen and trust each other's drum playing to base our rhythm on. It was important for us to work as a team as to not sound bad.

> Scotty [written response]: Rhythm is a very important key factor to stability because without rhythm things don't flow as easily and things can get chaotic. Rhythm brings harmony and allows people to work together . . . It helped me build better & new relationships because it brings people together into one by working on the same level all in rhythm.

> Timothy [written response]: The circle reminded me that this school, the church, and many teams are like that small drum circle. It takes many people to create something great. It also reminded me that I am a part of something greater than myself. Not just the drum circle, but many other things I do are a part of something greater than myself.

The writing from the adolescents' journal data illustrated that the session activities elicited consistent experience interpretations from the students that everyone has a part to play in society. The students related

---

15. Collected artifacts: May 1, 2018.

the concept of rhythm to dynamics needed in a team, society, the school, and the church. One student interpreted that these activities helped him recognize that he is part of something greater than a mere individual.

Throughout this session several emergent themes were present in the student-participants' written and verbal data on the topic of rhythm:

1. there is a natural rhythm of life

2. the importance of communication beyond words

3. that each individual has unique insights to contribute to the whole of the group.

From the activities and the follow-up reflections the student data indicated that there was recognition of natural rhythm in life. Harold wrote: "The drum circle was fully dependent on rhythm . . . Everyone had a part to play in the song . . . everyone is dependent on one another, and to me that is the definition of community."[16] Student data also indicated that communication is not just limited to verbal interaction; there is a lot of communication that exists through body movement and listening to others. Jerome wrote: "The musicians were constantly looking and watching each other in order to adjust or continue the rhythm."[17] The student data also indicated that each individual has a significant part or role within the whole group. Scotty wrote: "Rhythm brings harmony and allows people to work together . . . It helped me build better & new relationships because it brings people together into one by working on the same level all in rhythm."[18]

Media Examples for Adolescents

There are countless examples of songs and poems that can be used to offer adolescents a deeper sense of the symbols and themes to invite a dialogue for them to reflect on their life, purpose, and spirituality. As this topic is ever-changing, there is not enough opportunity to offer a suggestion for every situation before an example may go out of favor and another come into vogue. Hopefully, you will take the time to listen to an adolescent and learn about their favorite musicians; those tunes and poetic lyrics that move them into finding connection with the musician and culture. I also

16. Collected artifacts: May 1, 2018.
17. Collected artifacts: May 1, 2018.
18. Collected artifacts: May 1, 2018.

recommend to read Merton's poetry, as it offers an amazing insight into life and human expression. Thomas Merton was clearly a master of prose in his spiritual writings, but he was equally gifted in the rhythmic beauty and cadence found within the topics of his poetic works.

Practical Examen: Questions for Reflection

- Do *I* take time to listen to the music that adolescents are passionate about, to learn about their preferences?
- Have *I* contributed to encourage an adolescent to develop their skills as a musician or poet, and offer their talents to the best of their ability?
- Do *I* share my favorite musicians or poetic lyrics with my children, or adolescents, for them to better understand me?
- Have *I* explored Thomas Merton's poetry and analogies to gain a deeper insights into the world and humanity's part in it?
- Do *I* allow myself the time to read poetry and reflect on its meaning in my life, as well as my relationship with God?
- Have *I* volunteered to teach a musical instrument to someone else, or have *I* be open to learning a new skill like an instrument or writing poetry to better express myself to others?

10

The Arts Part II—Painting/Photography
The Appreciation of Beauty

Our being is not to be enriched merely by activity and experience as such.
Everything depends on the quality of our acts and our experiences.[1]

THOMAS MERTON ACKNOWLEDGED THAT experience alone was not sufficient for knowing and living in the world; it also depends on the reflection and quality offered to that experience. As mentioned previously,
Merton did not see himself as an accomplished athlete but he also did
not put forth the quality of time and effort needed to become an accomplished athlete. Merton is remembered for his spiritual writing, his
expansive exploration of God within the world and humanity; that was
what he devoted quality and effort to do well. He truly appreciated the
beauty of the God's presence throughout creation and the human person.
It is not an accident that Merton also developed an eye for beauty in art
and photography.

Ralph Eugene Meatyard, a close friend and local Kentucky photogra-
pher, reminisced in his eulogy for Thomas Merton:

> The last time I saw Tom was two days before he left for India. We
> dined for a long time over curry and talked about all the great times
> we had recently, laughed over a pratfall he took while participating

1. Merton, *No Man Is an Island*, 123.

in one of my pictures. We listened to his favorite records while he played the bongos. He showed me his new camera. Uncle Tom—as my children called him—gave my daughter Melissa his collection of his favorite publication—*Mad* magazine.[2]

This memory offered a clear picture of a man enjoying the beauty of life: photography, music, food, the humor of cartoon, and political satire. Merton lived life to the full and thoroughly appreciated all of its eccentric beauty. Much like a connoisseur of wine or art, who understands, engages, and brings to light the nuance of a piece of art or a fine wine, Thomas Merton brought to light the nuance of life itself. He was a connoisseur of the material and divine realities that bridged an insight into the totality of the beauty of human existence and brought it to a new appreciation through words, relationship, and art. There exist several examples of Thomas Merton's drawing and calligraphy that brings a refreshing insight into the artistic mind of Merton, the author and artist.[3] The following sketch of Gethsemani by Thomas Merton offers a sense of the tranquility of rural life surrounding the grounds, through the straight-lined images, while the middle of the sketch becomes dense and busy. One can only wonder what Merton intended through such a sketch.

2. Meatyard, "Eulogy of Thomas Merton," 57.
3. Lipsey, *Angelic Mistakes*.

This chapter will not only explore Merton's connection with such beauty but will explain why is it essential to instill that desire for quality of life and experience in the life of adolescents, who seek purpose and meaning in the contemporary world.

Understanding the Arts

Throughout the last decade and the rise of social media and digital technology educators have been challenged with an almost insurmountable task of creating a bridge between course material and the real-life experience of contemporary youth, especially in the regard of the value of human dignity. Experiences of digital photography, pixel editing, and perfecting a perspective have become the everyday standard. For example, when my three teenage daughters take a photograph on their iPhone it becomes a well-thought-out and hyper-analyzed process in their minds (as individuals and pseudo-artists). The era of the instant polaroid has evolved to a condition of necessary reliance on the use of countless Instagram or Snapchat filters, Photoshop editing, and artistic as well as personal value determined on the number of likes or comments a particular photo on social media receives within minutes or seconds.

How can ministers for adolescents engage a generation to the deep and holistic value of art and life when it is often only defined within such ideologically immediate expectations based on social media approval? To address and teach beyond the limited appreciation prominent in contemporary culture it is important to first reframe the perspective. Based on the artistic insights of Elliot Eisner, seen through the lens of Thomas Merton, one can create a foundation of approaching and understanding of the arts that can reach beyond the façade of passing cultural trends and offer a pedagogy grounded on appreciation of hope through ephemeral beauty and human variance of the arts as authentic human encounters.

Bridging Art and Education in a Contemporary Lens

Throughout his writings as an educator of the arts and connoisseur of pedagogy, Stanford professor Elliot Eisner offered insights into the nature of art and the human experience. Although not directly addressing the contemporary challenges of the social media and digital age, Eisner's writings offer a deep and penetrating appreciation of the very nature of humanity, and the need for education of the arts within a holistic human experience.[4] Elliot Eisner stated: "The arts are both a distillation of experience and a prototypal form through which we learn to experience the world."[5] It is from this foundation that his pedagogy can continue to speak beyond individual or generational limitations to bridge an authentic nature of humanity with appreciating art at its the purest and natural sense.

Education, at its very core, is a process and work of art.[6] The development of an adolescent is founded on the relationship of teacher and student that brings out, and gives meaning to, the gifts and talents of the other. It brings wholeness to the human experience and expression through emotion, nuance, and passion. Eisner stated that art education not only helps a student navigate and understand emotion, recognize multivariant meanings and solutions in life, but also offers a voice to aspects of the human condition that cannot be put into words.[7]

To develop such needed skills for lifelong success adolescents and adults need to become critics and connoisseurs of the context of their lives. Through being able to appraise, critique, and learn from defining experiences as well as living beyond personal or cultural stereotypes, prejudices,

or tragedies, students come to learn and grow through authentic human encounters. Art, through the form of poetry, film, lyrics, drama, and canvas can give rise to feelings, and often contextual meaning, to situations throughout our lives that words alone cannot do justice for.

Here an abstract drawing by Thomas Merton might elicit connection, emotions, feelings, or memories that words alone might not bring forth. For some individuals this drawing might be interpreted as a picture of the

4. See Eisner, *Arts and the Creation of the Mind.*

5. Eisner, "Educating the Whole Person," 40.

6. See Eisner, "Artistry in Education," 373–84.

7. See Eisner, *Arts and the Creation of the Mind.*

temptation in the Garden of Eden, with Adam and Eve on the right side of the Tree of the Knowledge of Good and Evil in the center (Gen 3). For other individuals, this sketch many be interpreted as individual dancing around a scene in nature. Whatever the interpretation art, and artistic expression, lays a contextual bridge for sharing and understanding one's human experience with another.

Ephemeral Beauty and Natural Variance: Appreciating Art through the Digital Mindset

Youth today are captivated with documenting and sharing their personal human experiences. Cell phones, tablets, and computer hard drives contain millions of bytes of dedicated storage for pictures, videos, and captured sound that define our lives. Digital picture-sharing applications utilizing social media have evolved into a multimillion-dollar industry through this desire to save and share our life through pictures and video.[8]

As an educator and parent, I hope that the consistent sharing of digital pictures is in some small way an illustration of the appreciation of natural variance of the human condition. There is a variation in all aspects of human life, from the most elemental and biological level to vastness of the galactic universe. Norms and variation come in all shapes and sizes. In the realm of art and the variance of art appreciation is an essential and indelible condition. Although some of us are extremely moved by a painting of Rembrandt or Caravaggio, a friend or neighbor may not care for the gritty emotion but might prefer the work of Warhol or Dali. Natural variance in the appreciation of art assumes that each individual is a de facto critic through personally comparing, contrasting, recollecting, and ultimately naturally entertaining an internal dialogue within the mind between preferential aspects of pieces of art.[9] What do you sense when looking at the following example of Merton's drawing of the crucifixion? What feelings does it evoke?

8. See Simon, "How Instagram Makes Money."
9. Eisner, "Objectivity in Educational Research," 9–15.

While recognizing natural variance in the world, though, there is a point to which we strive for a perfect quality, either in life or in the preferences of our mind. By trying to experience the "just right" or "perfect" fleeting moment an artist strives to capture ephemeral beauty. The Greeks used the term *kairos* to describe the right, opportune moment, a qualitative term describing a moment or decision that is more than mere serendipitous in nature. Similarly, Romans evolved the concept into the *carpe diem* mentality of seiz-

ing the day, which has become a consistent influence and motto throughout the Western consciousness. The motto has once again come to the forefront with a renewed energy in the YOLO, "you only live once," movement. YOLO has become a mantra throughout memes and social media trends, and has become a generational defense for behaviors that seize the moment, especially actions that are risky or dangerous such as in the extreme selfie trend. Natural variance and ephemeral beauty are both inherent aspects of culture, just manifested in new modes in the digital age for the adolescent mindset.

An Engaging Methodology: Educational Criticism and Connoisseurship

In his article "Questionable Assumptions About Schooling" Elliot Eisner offered suggestions for five dimensions needed for future educational reform.[10] The final dimension Eisner explored in the article focused on new and improved ways of evaluative practices in schools. I argue that this is needed more than ever in educational environments. Real life, working conditions, and family life do not resemble the protected confines of a classroom or a four-option multiple-choice assessment; classroom experiences do not offer an accurate representation of the consistent analysis and

10. Eisner, "Questionable Assumptions about Schooling," 648–57.

evaluative challenges of adulthood. To meaningfully prepare adolescents to be successful in life they need to develop skills such as: critical thinking, value judgments, literacy skills for appraisal of unfamiliar contexts, and evaluation of subjective and pseudo-objective natures which are inherent in an arts-based curriculum.

Elliot Eisner laid the groundwork for a qualitative inquiry method called educational criticism and connoisseurship.[11] This methodology structurally depends on four main aspects: description, interpretation, evaluation, and thematics.[12] These four components of the research methodology offer a parallel process of the natural process of basic education mechanics. The following example of using an arts-based medium to create a classroom dialogue on diversity and inclusion will utilize the process of description, interpretation, evaluation, and thematics.

Approaching Diversity and Inclusion using Educational Criticism and Connoisseurship

Inclusion and diversity are used as bywords for respect and tolerance throughout social media, on the news, and in schools and workplaces. I would bet, though, if you were to survey educators for a clear and concise definition of the terms there would likely be no consensus for the meaning of either term. Although inclusion and diversity are frequently used in the contemporary vocabulary both terms are packed with individual stereotypes, cultural expectations, and value judgments. It must be acknowledged that inclusion and diversity are loaded and passionate terms. Although inclusion and diversity are two of the most pressing concepts at the forefront of our culture, the terms are challenging and controversial because they demand an active response in individuals and groups—they are not passive terms.

The horrific recent national school-related tragedies are a painful reminder that society needs to purposefully and continuously create an environment of hope instead of one of fear. It is time to reassess and develop more deliberate activities that highlight the importance of the dignity of the human person, through the appreciation of diversity and inclusion. I would

11. Eisner, "Educational Connoisseurship and Criticism: Their Form and Functions in Educational Evaluation," 135–50; Flinders and Eisner, "Educational Criticism as a Form of Qualitative Inquiry," 341–57.

12. Uhrmacher et al., *Using Educational Criticism and Connoisseurship for Qualitative Research.*

like to offer two case studies, from an artistic lens, of individuals who became catalysts of inclusion and diversity, in the most authentic sense of the terms: Thomas Merton and Gord Downie. Although these individuals would not necessarily be considered traditional artistic exemplars their work and dedication to reconciliation and hope may offer foundations for a pedagogy toward a deeper understanding of inclusion and diversity for contemporary educators and a more holistic pedagogy based on human encounter.

Paving a New Way: Application with Adolescents

To create a catalyst for a pedagogical culture of inclusion and diversity, it is essential to look beyond traditional pedagogical methods and learn from historical examples that have succeeded in the type of change schools are searching for. I would like to purpose two exemplars: Thomas Merton and Gord Downie. Each of these individuals passionately desired change which was sparked by a national tragedy. Each individual used unique methods to bring hope to a culture of fear, unity to a culture of separation, and sense of purpose in the midst of negligence toward humanity. I hope that these two case studies will offer educators a renewed perspective to discuss inclusion and diversity in the classroom and explore further pedagogical methods to teach the necessity of the dignity of the human person.

Thomas Merton and the Bombing in Birmingham

The writings of Thomas Merton raised awareness of the dangers of war, poverty, social injustice, and human isolation. On September 15, 1963, a bombing occurred at the 16th Street Baptist Church in Birmingham, Alabama. The timed explosive device was left on the steps of the church by American white supremacist terrorists. More than twenty individuals were injured, but the bomb claimed the lives of four young girls who were between the ages of eleven and fourteen years old. To bring witness to the horror of the attack *LOOK Magazine* published an article about the attack and photos of the one of children who died during the explosion. The pictures of Carole Denise McNair, one of the victims, in common and ordinary activities (holding a doll, dressing up as a child, and waving to a camera), but all three pictures had a haunting and ephemeral beauty.[13]

13. Huie, "Death of an Innocent," 23–25.

Thomas Merton was so haunted by one of the photos that he kept the clipping from this magazine article, in his journal—as a constant reminder of the purity and innocence of someone who never learned how to hate.[14] Merton was also moved by the horrific attack to write a letter to the McNair family, as well as two poems entitled: "And the children of Birmingham" as well as "Picture of a black child with a white doll." What is clear from Merton's writing is that a new zealousness developed within his writings on nonviolence, an ardent call for renewal of the dignity of the human person, and the need for communal human unity came after 1963. Merton used the art of poetry and writing to move the hearts and minds of his generation for change during a time of social unrest. Merton's eloquent writings still inspire readers of the need for unity, not to be a bystander to violence but to become a determined and purposeful nonviolent resistor.

> PICTURE OF A BLACK CHILD WITH A WHITE DOLL (excerpt: stanza 1 and 5)
>
> Your dark eyes will never need to understand
> Our sadness who see you
> Hold that plastic glass-eyed
> Merchandise as if our empty-headed race
> Worthless full of fury
> Twanging and drooling in the southern light
> With guns and phantoms
> Needed to know love
>
> And what was ever darkest and most frail
> Was then your treasure-child
> So never mind
> They found you and made you a winner
> Even in most senseless cruelty
> Your darkness and childhood
> Became fortune yes became
> Irreversible luck and halo.[15]

Through these lines, inspired by a picture of the young girl in the magazine, Merton takes the reader to a sense of a myriad of emotions. It was evident that Merton himself was using poetry as a cathartic progress of grieving the death of Denise McNair but also a grief of the evil prominent within the country at that time. Merton's poetic words take the horrific

14. Merton, *Road to Joy*, 322.
15. Merton, "Picture of a Black Child with a White Doll," 626–27.

situation and realign the focus to the love and innocence of the young girl instead of focusing on the horrific act that shook the American culture.

To engage students in a similar study of the context offered above I also encourage adolescents to explore the historical context of the situation. By including YouTube interviews of the survivors' accounts of the Birmingham bombings or listening to Dr. Martin Luther King Jr.'s eulogy given for the children in such activities adolescents can come to a greater context of the events that inspired Merton's poetic response. By allowing the students to describe and interpret their feelings of the pictures from the original article, one of Merton's poems based on the event, and surrounding historical data the students will have the opportunity to speak of the natural variance of interpretations of those affected by the event as well as the ephemeral beauty of those touched by the tragedy to better understand the value and worth of all humanity.

Gord Downie and the Roots of Reconciliation with Cultural Genocide

Gord Downie was a poet, musician, and Canadian national icon. After reading a journalistic article from 1967 about the death of twelve-year-old Chanie Wenjack,[16] Gord Downie felt called to bring to light the tragic history plaguing Canada's past and to help establish hope and reconciliation. Though separated by several decades, Downie created lyrics and music, along with graphic art by Jeff Lemire, brought awareness to the controversial past and national tragedy that the indigenous residential school program inflicted upon First Nation children, through an artistic rendering of Chanie's life.[17]

The government inquest into the abuses of the resident schooling program uncovered that, over its one-hundred-year existence, an estimated 150,000 indigenous children were taken from their family homes and forced into the Canadian residential schooling program. The inquest also stated that over 4200 children died while being under the care of the residential school program across Canada.[18] Today, Downie's album and graphic novel are being used throughout classrooms and prison reading programs to become a catalyst for dialogues on inclusion and diversity to

16. Adams, "Lonely Death of Chanie Wenjack," 42–44.

17. See Downie and Lemire, *Secret Path.*

18. Johnson, "Centre for Truth and Reconciliation," para. 5; Levinson-King, "Canada Reveals Names," para. 11.

start a process of reconciliation in response to Canada's tragic past. *Secret Path* illustrates that the arts can, and should, be used as a bridge to seek reconciliation from past national tragedies and injustice, but more so to serve as a bridge for the future of inclusion and diversity especially for populations who have no other voice throughout the nation.

To engage students in a similar study of the context of the First Nation's plight have the students explore the historical context of the situation. Include the use of copies of the graphic novel accompanied by the recorded songs, as well as YouTube interviews of the survivors' accounts of the residential schools. Again, by having the students describe and interpret the historical context and its influence the students will have the opportunity to speak of the natural variance of interpretations of those affected by the event as well as the ephemeral beauty of those touched by the tragedy to better understand the value and worth of all humanity.

Action and the Arts: Where do we stand now?

As these examples have indicated the arts have the opportunity to offer tools for introducing curriculum concepts from a perspective of purposeful diversity and inclusion. Through these artistic mediums, students have the opportunity to describe, interpret, evaluate, and create themes that parallel their own diverse human encounters to connect history to the present and develop a greater awareness of the nature of community.

Inclusion is an essential part of the communal human condition, but how does diversity factor into that unity? I would propose that the truest sense of diversity has less to do with the external factors, such as race, nationality, gender, or other typical stereotypes but rather acknowledging the essence of human authenticity. Merton and Downie did not merely advocate for abstract concepts such as diversity or inclusion—they advocated for real-life human beings to be respected and honored as real-life human beings. Every student, teacher, minster, and school is endowed with unique and diverse talents, abilities, identities and legacies. Focusing on respecting the dignity and value of every human being and their unique identity, and cultural expression, might be a positive response to a culture of exclusion and fear that plagues the nation. The hope for a successful school is to unify diverse talents for holistic and communal success. May we truly know and welcome the stranger in our midst, because through that we will come to know our authentic selves

Practical Examen: Questions for Reflection

- Do *I* value the beauty of various art and media forms?

- Do *I* take time to experience the joy that an adolescent has in a particular piece of music, poetry, or digital clip?

- Have *I* been open to explore more artistic mediums to engage in various understanding of beauty?

- Have *I* taken time to interpret and evaluate various styles of art that I have experienced?

- Have *I* offered time for adolescents to evaluate and find trends in various pieces of art that define their life?

- Do *I* take time to recognize the beauty in nature and the artistic works of God in my life?

11

Advocacy

A Call for Others

The idea of *kairos*—the time of urgent and providential decision—is something characteristic of Christianity, a religion of decisions in time and in history. Can Christians recognize their *kairos*? Is it possible that when the majority of Christians become aware that "the time has come" for a decisive and urgent commitment, the time has, in fact, already run out?[1]

ONE OF THE STRONGEST and most remembered aspects of the life and writings of Thomas Merton was his deep call of advocacy for others. He often wrote and reflected that humanity did not find fulfillment or happiness alone, but through community. Through relationship with others each human being comes to find its truest nature. At face value these statements may seem like an oxymoron coming from a hermit of the rural Kentucky, but advocacy is a foundational theme of Merton's poetry, prose, and numerous correspondences.

From advocacy of the Catholic rituals and traditions in *Seven Storey Mountain*, nonviolence in reflection and awareness of the horror of the Second World War in the "Original Child Bomb," advocacy of the Civil Rights Movement through poems such as "And the Children of Birmingham," and advocacy and awareness of ecumenism and interreligious dialogue with

1. Merton, "Religion and Race in the United States," 218.

Eastern spirituality throughout his playful and starstruck journal entries preparing to meet the Dalai Lama, Merton advocated for divserse expressions of humanity.[2] No matter the topic, Merton's passion and advocacy were an ever-present aspect of his charm as an author.

Similarly, adolescence is a time defined by advocacy. As youth mature toward young adulthood there is a natural development and desire for deep callings and commitments of advocacy and beliefs. In recent years social media has given a platform for numerous examples of adolescent advocacy—although not always becoming viral sensations, these moments become bound by *kairos*—a time of urgent and providential decision-making. The following were just a few viral examples of youth prominent advocacy.

Examples of Youth Advocacy

In March 2018, in response to the frequent history of school shootings and, at that time, the most recent school shooting in Parkland, Florida on February 14, 2018, a national school walkout was organized as a response to gun violence.[3] The movement was critically acclaimed by several media sources as a positive and needed example of social change led by adolescents.

A second example from early 2019 involved Catholic school youth that developed into a confrontation at the Lincoln Memorial during the conclusion of March for Life and the Indigenous Peoples March. At the Memorial, while waiting for buses, adolescent students were engaged in an escalated convergence between members from the Black Hebrew Israelites and Native American activists. During the altercation groups of adolescent students began to advocate their perspectives in opposition to the comments from the other groups. This event became national news, and the actions of the students were immediately and harshly condemned across the nation. The situation was later explored in a more complete context which cast a much more favorable light upon the actions of the students than initially thought.

A third example could be seen in the emotional testimony of Greta Thunberg before the United Nations in September 2019. Originally a school strike for climate change, Thunberg's movement evolved into a movement

2. Merton, *Asian Journals*, 100–102.

3. Correal et al., "March for Our Lives Highlights."

for global awareness, authorship, a short-list potential recipient of a Nobel Prize, and *TIME Magazine* Person of the Year for 2019.[4]

These examples offer brief illustrations that adolescents desire to stand their ground, be defenders of their beliefs, and be social advocates even though that advocacy may or may not be for a perspective or belief that coincides with mainstream perspectives. As stated in the Book of the Prophet Jeremiah: "But the LORD said to me, "Do not say, 'I am only a boy'; for you shall speak to all to whom I send you" (Jer. 1:7).

Advocacy: The Roots of Community

Advocacy is one of the primary trends that has been acknowledged to define the maturation process during adolescence, and is an essential component of understanding adolescent spirituality. Advocacy can be described as the investment of time and energy on behalf of a believed cause or endeavor. As illustrated above, adolescents believe and support activities that bring meaning and connection to their lives. Throughout this age of maturation, and boundary testing, an adolescent may support causes that seem, or are, in direct opposition to previous held traditions or expectations of their parents. An adolescent is in the process of seeking truth within the context of their understanding in contrast to previous held doctrines or teachings that others might prefer them to assume without challenge.

Advocacy is an essential but challenging aspect to comprehend and form throughout the development within adolescence due to various peer groups and searching for an identity and belief system. It nonetheless lays a foundation and is deeply connected to maturation into adulthood. The twentieth-century priest and educator Luigi Giussani reminded the church that education is based on experience which essentially includes a dimension of risk; risk on behalf of the student as well as on behalf of the educator.[5] For adolescents to mature, it is important to allow such risk for growth, even through painful experiences so that the individual can become refined and strengthened for adulthood and face future life challenges with courage, fortitude, and authenticity.

Thomas Merton was well aware of the risk involved with authentic advocacy. Advocacy can become polarizing upon the identity of a community,

---

4. Alter et al., "TIME 2019 Person of the Year."

5. See Giussani, *Risk of Education.*

but it is the nature of labeling things through polar extremes that is at the root of unhealthy relationship with God:

> This crazy belief in people who are absolutely good and people who are absolutely bad (the stock in trade of totalitarian society) is inseparable from lack of belief in God, and to me the frightful outcry, scandal, pious horror, and generally unrealistic attitude people have taken toward the case, is simply characteristic of a country that knows nothing of God.[6]

Merton stated that life is much more complex than merely a system of polar opposites, wrong actions and right actions. Merton's advocacy and desire for unity in heart, mind, and community in response to hatred, violence, and war have come to endure as part of his long-lasting legacy as a spiritual writer. Merton's advocacy took the form of commentary on social activism during the Civil Rights Movement. Through correspondence, poems, and short essays, Merton offered spiritual insight on world events involving war and examining cultural racism. Some of his most famous and poignant writings of advocacy and challenge include topics on nuclear war and the effects of the bombs on the minds of hearts of the world, reflections on the life and sanity of the actions of Nazi S.S. Lieutenant-colonel Adolf Eichmann, and the collected correspondence of Merton throughout times of crisis. One such letter written by Merton from April 1964 acknowledged the need and cost of living and writing as a Catholic advocate:

> The writer who has "influence" on the people who really need to read him must have something important to say, and something that is important *now* or perhaps tomorrow, later than now. And he must want to say it to the men of his time, perhaps even to others later. But it must be a bit desperate if it is going to get out at all. And if it is desperate, it will be opposed. Hence no writer who has anything important to say can avoid being opposed or criticized. Thus the writer who wants to—let us say reach, or help rather than influence people—must suffer for the truth of his witness and for love of the people he is reaching. Otherwise his communion with them is shallow and without life. The real writer lives in deep communion with his readers, because they share in common sufferings and desires and needs that are *urgent*.[7]

---

6. For further context see Merton, "Letter to Charles Van Doren, November 7, 1959"; and Daggy, "Thomas Merton & the Quiz Show Scandal," 4–11.

7. Merton, "Letter to Lorraine, April 17, 1964," 167.

The legacy of Merton cannot be separated from his passion, search for the authentic-self, and advocacy of the dignity of the human person through advocacy of social justice. Here Merton indicated that these three longings: self-discovery, passion, and advocacy are bound together within deep communion with others. Merton's life, through his writings, offered a common experience to the challenges and searching nature of an adolescent.

Contemporary Adolescents: Searching for an Ethical Perspective

As mentioned previously in this text there has been much research into the beliefs and perspectives of adolescents toward religion through the data collected from the NSYR. One of the most illuminating aspects of the study was the moral trends that evolved from the interview data of the youth. Scholars stated that the primary view espoused by adolescents that emerged from the NSYR data could be best summarized as Moral Therapeutic Deism.[8]

Moral Therapeutic Deism was defined as a moral lens that centers on the emotional experience of feeling good, exemplified by acting nice, but remaining at a distance with God until something important in one's life is required.[9] The data collected throughout the study also indicated that Moral Therapeutic Deism was exemplified by individualistic view focused more on the desires of one's individual feelings and preferences rather than the personal need for community and relationship, for God or others; if an individual is good, that individual will have a happy life now and in the afterlife. Ultimately, this moral perspective easily places value on the worth of others merely as utilitarian relationships. Although the NSYR data and subsequent analysis indicated that adolescents stated that religion is a good thing, they very rarely tend to engage such beliefs in their daily lives.

Now, almost two decades removed from the first collection of the NSYR data, further evolving trends are emerging from adolescent culture. In the wake of the technological boom there has been less of an appreciation for traditional religious affliction and structure. The emerging trend is a religious affiliation that espouses being: spiritual, but not religious. In 2012, YouTube user Jefferson Bethke became a viral sensation and social media celebrity with his spoken-word slam poem "Why I Hate Religion,

8. See: Smith and Denton, *Soul searching*.

9. See: Smith and Denton, *Soul searching*; and Dean, *Almost Christian*.

But Love Jesus," which currently has close to 34.5 million views to date.[10] Bethke's central claim was that religion, the governance, standards, and rituals, have become a corrupt distortion of the original message of Jesus. The four-minute clip points out, through short phrases, the seemingly hypocritical nature of religious institutions through rhyme and rhythm. As a response to the mass popularity to Betkhe's clip Catholic religious leaders attempted to respond using social media as well, but Betkhe's initial clip's popularity and engaging style had much more cultural exposure.[11]

Through its witness the church firmly acknowledges that the foundation for adolescent spirituality and advocacy is Jesus himself.[12] Throughout the Gospels Jesus's actions exemplify advocacy: compassion and inclusion of the outcast—such as the stories of Zacchaeus (Luke 19:1–10), the woman caught in the act of adultery (John 8:1–11), and the woman at the well (John 4:4–42); healing and restoring dignity of the sick and those in poverty such as the healing of the paralytic (Matt 9:1–8; Mark 2:1–12; Luke 5:17–26) and the woman with the hemorrhage (Mark 5:25–34); and offering wholeness for the possessed and isolated sinful, such as the expulsion of the demoniacs (Mark 5:1–13) and the man born blind (John 9:1–12). Advocacy for those individuals on the fringe and outskirts of society is part of the drive of humanity, a deep yearning for equality in an unjust world.

Merton's Ethical Response to Reclaim Human Dignity— Christian Humanism

Advocacy for the dignity and worth of humanity is essential today. It can be a challenge to teach adolescents the direct connection between advocacy and the dignity and worth of humanity without tangible, real-life examples. In his writings, Thomas Merton explored Christian Humanism as a tangible ethical perspective to bridge the knowledge of dignity and worth of humanity with real-life application in a contemporary context. Christian Humanism is an ethical perspective that states that all humanity has dignity and worth, that individual freedom exists founded on that dignity, and that human fulfillment subsists in the attainment of ultimate happiness,

10. See: Betkhe, "Why I Hate Religion, But Love Jesus."

11. See Barron, "Bishop Barron on 'Why I Hate Religion, But I Love Jesus'"—500 thousand views; and Spirit Juice, "Why I Love Religion, and Love Jesus"—roughly one million views (as of November 2019).

12. *Joy of Adolescent Catechesis*, 7.

which is found in living authentically based on the gospel message of Jesus of Nazareth, in light of the incarnation.[13] The roots of Christian Humanism can be traced to the Early Church theologians: Justin Martyr, Tertullian, and Augustine, but is most recognized in ethical writings of Erasmus of Rotterdam and Petrarch.[14] Today this ethical perspective has reemerged and can be used to best describe the themes and writings of John Paul II, G. K. Chesterton, Flannery O'Connor, Dorothy Day, Thomas Merton, and Martin Luther King Jr., as well as many other twentieth-century advocates of the dignity and value of human life.[15]

Thomas Merton wrote directly on the call for greater awareness of Christian Humanism as an ethical view in several essays. Although Merton did not completely devote his writing to the topic of Christian Humanism, the vast majority of Merton's themes and writings follow the tenets of a Christian Humanist ethic by focusing on the dignity and worth of all of humanity and the search for the authenticity of one's self that is inherently linked and made sacred from the incarnation.[16] "Christianity can and must contribute something of its own unique and irreplaceable insights into the value of man, not only in his human nature, but his inalienable dignity as a free person."[17] Merton believed that through the incarnation, a Christian ethic derives from a full recognition of the nature and dignity of humanity, which lays a foundation on the human person and societal relationships. Merton stated:

> Our modern world cannot attain to peace, and to fully equitable social order, merely by application of laws which act upon man, so to speak, from outside himself. The transformation of society begins within the person. It begins with the maturing and opening out of personal freedom in relation to other freedoms . . . This means a capacity to be open to others as persons, to desire for others all that we know to be needful for ourselves, all that is required for the full growth and even the temporal happiness of a fully personal existence.[18]

13. See Franklin and Shaw, *Case for Christian Humanism.*

14. See Shaw et al., *Readings in Christian Humanism.*

15. Zimmermann, "Introduction," 1–15.

16. For further context see Merton, *Love and Living*, 135–232; as well as Moses, *Divine Discontent*, 203–4.

17. Merton, "Christian Humanism," 138.

18. Merton, "Christian Humanism in the Nuclear Era," 154–55.

Merton argued that ultimate happiness was the goal of humanity. In his correspondence with adolescents the desire and encouragement for happiness became a frequent theme. Interestingly it was included in his first response to Sr. Lorenz's high school class in 1949 and echoed in the final letters addressed to Suzanne Butorovich.

Merton: A Life of Advocacy in Action

From his youth to his death Merton constantly engaged, and was deeply aware of, the challenges of the American culture of the twentieth century, from its historical influences to the contemporary perspectives of his day. Merton's writings illustrated his ability to draw connections of a human consciousness found in the transcendent realities that bound humanity as a whole, from Ancient Greek literature to the social movement of nonviolence in the 1960s. Merton offered a creative perspective into the mystery of God and one's vocation in relationship with God. He deeply believed that this type of vocational relationship with God satisfied and gave meaning to all other relationships. The following picture shows Merton in conversion with peers and nonviolent advocates, including Daniel and Philip Berrigan, in 1962.

Thomas Merton did not shy away from controversy in his commentaries on world events, such the arms race, American racism, the Vietnam War, or national scandals. He was not influenced to write his commentaries because of bandwagoning or readership, he saw himself as a nonconformist. In an interview with Thomas P. McDonnell Merton stated: "My most unpopular opinions have been those in which I have come out against the Bomb, the Vietnam war, and in fact our whole social system."[19] Merton was not concerned about popularity but felt called to advocate for purposeful change of societal structures and advocated against beliefs that dehumanized and perpetuated the objectification of the human person. On multiple occasions, in his journals, Merton labeled himself as a Christian anarchist; a label similarly used by Dorothy Day and the Catholic Workers' Movement to express the belief that secular political systems need to be changed or removed because of their corrupt nature, and that the only allegiance one should truly have is to the teachings of Jesus.

Advocacy: Application with Adolescents

To help adolescents learn about the advocacy beyond mere sound bites and perceptions formed by viral sensations it is important to consistently offer clear and virtuous examples of advocacy, especially throughout the church. Where to begin? It is easy to rely on American exemplars such as Martin Luther King Jr., or the global face of international advocacy for the poor and rejected by Mother Teresa of Calcutta and the Sisters of Charity. To really reach adolescents it takes risk to explore the topics of their interest and advocacy—it will involve a challenge on the part of the adult to respect the perspectives and beliefs of the adolescent to start such a dialogue because it will force the adult to reassess their own held traditions and perspectives. As Merton offered:

> The dread of being open to the ideas of others generally comes from our hidden insecurity about our own convictions. We fear that we may be 'converted'—or perverted by a pernicious doctrine. On the other hand, if we are mature and objective in our open-mindedness, we may find that by viewing things from a basically different perspective—that of our adversary—we discover our own truth in a new light and are able to understand our own ideal more realistically.[20]

---

19. McDonnell, "Interview with Thomas Merton," 34.
20. Merton, "Blessed are the Meek," 214.

Today's adolescents are searching for meaning in civil social activism, through topics like global warming and care for creation; identity issues and social equality. The challenge is that many topics that have become quick talking points in the media and entertainment would need much more time and conversation than a sound bite. Such topics did not originate from our society or from the recent past, but have been part of the human consciousness for over a millennium. It is important to help an adolescent recognize their connection with the great history of human advocacy which will help find balance and clarity to historical reality.

In the midst of these changes and challenges, and political polarization, our culture is drawn to search for a magic bullet, or that one thing that will put all things right. Hollywood is very aware of this deep desire for an advocate and unifying savior for our world. Over the past decade the top-grossing films have mostly involved the power and advocacy of superheros, such as Marvel, DC, and countless television shows and spin-offs, whose plots are based on apocalyptic scenes of heroes fighting to save humanity from some type of global danger or chaos.

This captivation with all things surrounding chaos, and the end of the world, is not all that different from the culture of Jesus. Messianic Jews under the control of the Babylonians, Greeks, or Romans were waiting for a prophesied savior, and some continue to wait even today. Christians also await the return of the Christ. In their original context, though, the readings for today offer a sign of hope for those who were abandoned by their leaders, those suffering for their faith, and those who had no other help but God.

Although Scripture passages, especially during the season of Advent, discuss the signs of the times, some frightening and some more comforting, these visions ultimately are signs of hope for the faithful and comfort for the persecuted. We can have confidence in this hope because through these readings we are given the end of the story—the good guy wins. He has already won! The question at the heart of these readings is an honest one, though: why does the fear of chaos have us looking for a savior beyond the Lord? "Who is like you, O LORD, among the gods? Who is like you, majestic in holiness, awesome in splendor, doing wonders?" (Exod 15:11).

In his reflection, "The Time of the End is Time of No Room," Merton ironically reflects that the end times will mirror the time of the birth of Jesus; there will be no room for God. Like the lack of room in the inn in Luke's Gospel, our hearts will be so full for material things that we will have no room for Christ. Thankfully, recognizing the importance of advocacy in maturation and adolescent spirituality reminds all of us of the importance of the other. For it is through the example of others that a person learns how to become a full human being. Our life is a call for others.

Practical Examen: Questions for Reflection

- How much time do *I* listen to the interests and concerns of adolescents?

- Am *I* living in *kairos* to engage adolescents as advocates of the gospel?

- Have *I* ever thought about how, and why, adolescents seek relationships in social media and video games rather than engage with a present and tangible community?

- Thomas Merton indicated that happiness is the ultimate goal for our existence—how am *I* living for happiness and witness of happiness for others in my life, especially adolescents?

- How have *I* created, invited, or allowed an adolescent to engage in an adult decision process where that young adult can experience the accountability and responsibility of situations of maturation?

- Why might it be easier to become an obstacle to the growth of an adolescent than to allow that young adult to mature with adult decision-making experiences?

12

Bullying

Recognizing the Dignity and Worth of all Humanity

We have to learn to commune with ourselves before we can communicate with other men and with God. A man who is not at peace with himself necessarily projects his interior fighting into the society of those he lives with, and spreads a contagion of conflict all around him.[1]

THOMAS MERTON'S SPIRITUAL INSIGHTS continue to offer thoughts for reflection well after his life and times. They continue to offer reflection into the deepest core of human experiences. In his autobiography, *The Seven Storey Mountain*, Merton recounted several experiences of his involvement with bullying, as a victim and as a bully. Merton's recollections of such events were not recorded as isolated situations from his past, but were analyzed through the lens of a mature spirituality exploring the isolation and separation that was created between the bully and victim, which reflected on his experience in either the role of bully or victim.

Merton wrote about his regret regarding his own actions as a youth and reflected on the rejection that occurred from his actions. He was consciously aware of the isolation and rejection of communion that occurs as a consequence of bullying behavior, and is the complete opposite of Merton's view of the core human desire of love, community, and the suffering and

1. Merton, *No Man Is an Island*, 120–21.

pain that comes from the rejection of that inherent desire. His writings offer insights that do not explain the trauma of bullying but plumb into the consequences that bullying behavior can leave upon bullies and victims, especially from a spiritual perspective.

The Epidemic of Adolescent Bullying

Bullying is a common experience for adolescents in culture. It has become a well-documented epidemic in schools, the workplace, politics, and the broad society through social stereotypes throughout the last two centuries.[2] While some critics have stated that bullying is just part of human nature, recent scholars have advocated that bullying behaviors are personal choices and should not be justified as merely a natural human response. Bullying behaviors have become so commonplace in societal structure that many actions have been justified to not be that harmful to others, such as stereotypical acceptance of racism and sexism of nineteenth- and twentieth-century America. It is necessary to not only address such deep-seeded societal examples as Merton often did but also expose the destructive nature of bullying that affect the hearts and attitudes of adolescents.

Violent actions, derogatory language, and ostracism in adolescent relationships have become commonplace.[3] In their eye-opening volume of school, internet, and workplace bullying, Christa Boske and Azadeh Osanloo argued that our culture can no longer be permitted to dismiss or neglect action toward addressing adolescent bullying; bullying behaviors ought to be recognized as an immediate concern because of such grave consequences for adolescents, such as isolation, depression, and suicidal ideation.[4]

The connection between bullying and suicide has become so prominent that it has been used as a plotline of the popular novel and Netflix multi-season series adaptation, *13 Reasons Why*. Researchers Ayers et al. indicated that after the Netflix series originally aired Google search engine

---

2. For a specific context on contemporary issues on bullying see Boske and Osanloo, *Students, Teachers, and Leaders Addressing Bullying in Schools*; Huggins, "Stigma Is the Origin of Bullying," 166–96.

3. See Wiseman, *Queen Bees & Wannabees*, 2009; Boske and Osanloo, *Students, Teachers, and Leaders Addressing Bullying in Schools*, 2015.

4. Boske and Osanloo, "Uncomfortable Truths," xiii–xxiii; and Boske, "Bullied," 1–22; and Shaffer and Gordon, *Why Girls Talk and What They're Really Saying*, 10–13.

queries regarding suicide lyrics and ideation more than doubled.[5] In 2019, the first billion dollar-grossing R-rated film, *The Joker* brought to the forefront, through a psychological exploration, the motivations of the infamous DC comic villain, the Joker. The plot of the film follows the evolution of his murderous rampage, as direct revenge and consequences from the effects of physical, emotional, and psychological maladies from severe and societally accepted bullying behavior.

The frequency and persistence of adolescent bullying in schools as well as the psychological distress, physical exhaustion, and self-harm present in victims of bullying behaviors have become a growing concern. The Centers for Disease Control and Prevention recently reported that 20 percent of high school students reported being bullied on school grounds, while 16 percent reported being bullied over the Internet within the previous year.[6] Boske and Osanloo argued that such reported data on bullying should be considered gross underestimates. Students often do not report all incidents of bullying to school faculty. Reasons for large numbers of unreported incidents in most survey data often include fear of further bullying, not wanting to be seen as a tattletale, not trusting adults to resolve the situation in a positive way, or trying to resolve the situation on their own. Erin Leonard, a psychotherapist and researcher on adolescent health and behavior, stated that bullying should be acknowledged as an epidemic indicating that up to 83 percent of girls and 79 percent of boys report being bullied at school or online throughout the course of their schooling years.[7]

The Roots of Bullying Behavior

Bullying is often defined by scholars through two forms of bullying behavior: physical and verbal. Actions of physical aggression perpetrated by a bully upon a victim are the most common images associated with bullying behavior. Physical bullying behavior can range from shoving, cutting, and burning, to predatory behavior such as sexual touching or stalking, or extreme assaulting behaviors such as broken bones or homicides. Physical bullying often is found through an inequality in physical appearance or

5. Ayers et al., "Internet Searches for Suicide Following the Release of 13 Reasons Why."

6. Centers for Disease Control and Prevention, "Youth Risk Behavior Surveillance."

7. Leonard, *Battle Against Juvenile Bullying.*

physical power of the bully over the victim, based on differences in a disability, height, weight, or gender.

Although bullying behavior is easily recognized and identified in examples of physical abuse it is also experienced through verbal abuse, stereotyping, stigmatizing, or personal or social prejudice. Verbal abuses such as vulgarities based on race, sexuality, sexual expression, and physical appearances, as well as social status are slowing recognized as legitimate forms of bullying. Repeated verbal assaults that lead to the alienation or seclusion of an individual from a group are also identified as bullying behaviors. Sarcasm and shaming are also common forms of verbal harassment, especially in environments of social media. Unfortunately, these verbal events are not usually associated with bullying behavior because they often take a more culturally rationalized form, such as sexualized jokes or disparaging terms or gestures.

The common trends associated with a clear definition of bullying behavior include the following two aspects: repetitive actions of aggression and an imbalance of power between the bully and victim.[8] It is important to recognize that resolving bullying behavior is an extremely complicated process. Although there are countless factors involved with adolescent bullying behaviors the following three factors will serve as an introduction to its complexity: peer pressure and the desire for peer acceptance; self-esteem and personal insecurities; and abuse or humiliation.

Peer Pressure

One of the contributing factors within adolescent bullying is the power of ideological group dynamics found in peer pressure or cliques.[9] For adolescents, peer groups offer a sense of inclusion and a feeling of worth. This is not a new concept. It is acknowledged that the human race is social by nature and inherently desires to connect with others.[10] As an adolescent begins to mature toward young adulthood popularity within a peer group, acceptance of ideas, number of friends, and response of inclusion in peer communities become a self-metric of worth and value. When excluded

---

8. See Boske and Osanloo, "Uncomfortable Truths," xv; Huggins, "Stigma Is the Origin of Bullying," 169.

9. Classic examples of peer pressure and cliques can be seen in the film *Mean Girls* (2004), as well as in Wiseman, *Queen Bees & Wannabees*, 2009.

10. See Merton, *No Man Is an Island*.

from group and communal activities, an adolescent believes that they have little worth or value in the eyes of others.

When a peer group is founded based on the exclusion of others, a dynamic within the group will create a separation between the like-minded group members and those who are seen as different to that group. Merton mentioned the foundations of this type of group ideology when explaining the plague of racism to junior high student Besti Baeten:

> [People] instinctively censor their own ideas of themselves and others: the traits they *like*, they tend to see in themselves and in their friends. The traits they don't like they see in strangers, aliens, and those who are different from themselves. Then they feel they can punish these other people for being different, bad, or wrong, etc. Instead of having to admit evil in themselves, and having to live with it, they project it on others.[11]

Mirroring Merton's language, scholar and nursing professor Mike Huggins also referred to those separated by a clique, as the *other*; an individual who does not embody the community norms and is considered a threat to the group identity.[12] Over time, when this negative group identity strengthens among the members of the clique, the separation of the stigmatized outcast widens until the other is not only ridiculed for their lack of inclusion but becomes dehumanized in word and action by the clique.

Self-Esteem

A second significant contributing factor regarding adolescent bullying is self-esteem. In search of self-discovery, adolescents test and challenge previously taught doctrines and dogmas to find their personal convictions and moral systems. Some of the decisions and traditions that adolescents test during this period can be perceived by their parents or mainstream culture as taboo. The emotional struggle of conformity to cultural expectations does not leave an adolescent unaffected, but plays a significant role in their life and choices. Many adolescents do not know how to control their feelings or know the expected or proper response in life situations, as a result, adolescents will often create a mask and develop a new persona to become liked by others. Merton addressed the danger of this dichotomous identity:

11. Merton, "Letter to Besti Baeten, October 2, 1967," 358.
12. See Huggins, "Stigma Is the Origin of Bullying."

Alienation begins when culture divides me against myself, puts
a mask on me, gives me a role I may or may not want to play.
Alienation is complete when I become completely identified with
my mask, totally satisfied with my role, and convince myself that
any other identity or role is inconceivable.[13]

From being cut from an athletic team, the end of a relationship, family
issues like divorce, or the death of a loved one, adolescents can become
emotionally overwhelmed without possessing the discipline and neuro-
biological development to control their actions and emotional outbursts
that can seriously affect their relationships with others. As an adolescent
becomes emotionally hurt, an internal loop can develop and evolve to consistently shape the identity of the adolescent; defining their worth, and the
way he or she believes others value their presence.

Without developing healthy and mature ways of coping, which acknowledge their authentic dignity, an adolescent can turn to aggressive solutions to stop the emotional pain or revenge, such as cutting, hurting others
physically or verbally, or in extreme forms in suicidal ideation or homicide.
Since these types of responses are not socially accepted the adolescent will
feel even more isolated from society and will try to negotiate their feelings
with the advice of like-minded peers instead of someone with more mature
advice. As the behavior becomes more unacceptable socially, the adolescent
will often isolate further and further, distancing their ability to receive proper
guidance and help from an established or traditional community.

Abuse and/or Humiliation

Scholars have also indicated that bullying and violent actions may develop
from cyclic abusive events that an adolescent had previously experienced.
Adolescents learn how to develop socially acceptable behaviors from interaction with others. When moments of humiliation, or physical or emotional violence, are experienced in repetition an adolescent will develop a
malformed view of morality and social norms. After experiences of neglect
or abuse the world is often interpreted as a threatening and fearful place
for an adolescent. It is extremely difficult to understand the motivations
and mindset of an adolescent negotiating abuse if an individual does not
interpret the world in a similar hostile way.

13. Merton, *Literary Essays of Thomas Merton*, 381.

Merton addressed this factor of cyclic abuse and violence within the perspective of society in a communal letter distributed to a collective of his friends and frequent correspondences. He indicated that the growing cycle of violence of 1968, referencing the assassinations of Martin Luther King Jr. and Robert Kennedy, mirrored a cycle where although there is violence and an outcry against violence, it cycles back to violence again. In his mid-summer 1968 letter circulated to close friends he stated that as a culture we often harm and destroy the very things we profess to believe we need and ought to admire.[14] Cliques, self-esteem, and cyclic examples of abuse can distort the authentic recognition of the dignity of the human person, and instead of filling that individual with a longing for wholeness an adolescent

14. Merton, "Midsummer 1968 Circular Letter to Friends," 115–17.

can easily develop a life of unhealthy, disordered, and troubling goals causing harm to their self or others.

Merton: Experiences of Bullying

In his writings, Merton offered testimony to instances where he was at times a bully and when he was a victim of the bullying behaviors of others. The following vignettes serve as a few instances of Merton's experiences of bullying behaviors as well as the spiritual reflection that Merton offered upon those situations.

One of Merton's clearest memories of his younger brother, John Paul, was an event where he physically bullied and forcibly rejected his brother. Merton explained that while he and his neighborhood friends were building a fort, from which they purposefully excluded the younger children of the neighborhood:

> We severely prohibited John Paul and Russ's little brother Tommy and their friends from coming anywhere near us. And if they did try to come and get into our hut, or even look at it, we would chase them away with stones.[15]

Merton acknowledged that the purposeful rejection of John Paul and physical distance was used to demonstrated his superiority over the younger neighborhood children. As he continued his memory John Paul did not leave after being hit by the stones but remained at a safe distance and just continued to stare towards the fort—isolated, rejected, and confused; full of anger, offense, emptiness, and deep sadness.[16]

Merton also recalled experiences when he was the victim of physical and verbal bullying. The experience of the rejection he received in school remained with him, even as an adult.[17] As an eleven-year-old student in France, Merton recounted that his anxiousness and lack of fluency of the French language on his first day of school caused him to become paralyzed in the midst of his peers. The ridicule and isolation he received from his peers at the school stayed with him. Merton discussed being physically pushed, pulled,

---

15. Merton, *Seven Storey Mountain*, 25.

16. Merton, *Seven Storey Mountain*, 26.

17. He parallels such abuse he received as a small taste, as a foreigner in French and English schools, to experiences of racism of children in the 1960s. See Merton, *Road to Joy*, 345.

kicked, and shouted at during this schooling period: "I knew for the first time in my life the pangs of desolation and emptiness and abandonment."[18]

Again, Merton spiritualized these events of bullying which left him feeling empty and depressed. In his narrative Merton offered another illustration of a clique and peer ideology through the actions of his peers. Although the students at his school were mild and peaceful as individuals, when together a certain group of boys came together, they acted as though they were possessed by a diabolical spirit, like a wolf-pack.[19]

Group aggression, bullying, and scapegoating were not only discussed in Merton's early writings but also became a prominent theme throughout his commentaries on acts of social injustice throughout his life. One clear example that illustrated Merton's complete frustration and scathing view of cultural bullying involved the son of a close friend, Charles Van Doren.[20] In 1957, Charles Van Doren was a contestant on the nationally syndicated television game show, *Twenty-One.* Throughout his successful fourteen-week winning streak on the game show, Charles received national notoriety for his knowledge and winnings.[21]

In 1959, though, Charles, along with other game-show participants, were implicated in a national scandal of the fraud by the television quiz shows.[22] Charles had to testify before Congress during the federal investigation.[23] Because of his notoriety, academic profile, and his incriminating testimony Charles became a national scapegoat.[24] On November 7, 1959, Merton wrote to Charles Van Doren after the verdict to offer encouragement in the wake of the isolation and stigmatization that Van Doren experienced from the wake of the national scandal:

18. Merton, *Seven Storey Mountain*, 54.

19. Merton, *Seven Storey Mountain*, 55.

20. Charles was the eldest son of one of Merton's Columbia professors, mentors, and lifelong friends, Mark Van Doren. For further context see: Merton, *Road to Joy*, 3–55. There are also several partial sections of letters from Mark Van Doren to Merton collected chronologically throughout Van Doren, *The Selected Letters of Mark Van Doren.*

21. Charles was on the cover of TIME magazine, 1957. For additional context see: Van Doren, *The Selected Letters of Mark Van Doren*, 220.

22. For additional context about the scandal and its relationship with Merton and the Van Doren Family, see Daggy, "Thomas Merton & the Quiz Show scandal," 4–11; The scandal was later loosely dramatized for the plot in the Academy Award-nominated 1994 film *Quiz Show* directed by Robert Redford.

23. See "Investigation of Television Quiz Shows."

24. Van Doren, "All the Answers."

This is actually a great moral and psychological problem in our country I think. It is actually what we are doing as a nation in the world today: we are being deceptive, and more than that we are being aggressive, selfish, unjust, pharasaically [*sic*] pious etc, and counting on our sincerity and subjective 'good will', our feeling that we are nice guys, to get us by. It scares me to death, it is terrible. And of course it is in me, as well as in everybody. We are all you, at the moment, and there is no consolation in the fact except for those of us who may be able to see the fact. The sad part is that most people refuse to see that you are all of them. In rejecting you, those who have rejected you have rejected what they ought to love and cherish in themselves.[25]

Merton clearly indicated that the emotional isolation of the American public's attitude to the scandal stigmatized Charles, while also dehumanizing him and negating his previous achievements. Similar to his reflections in *The Seven Storey Mountain*, Merton's view of the situation offers an important perspective into the nature of bullying behavior: when one person becomes isolated from the whole community, everyone within the group suffers because of that isolation. This perspective, alluded to by Merton, which recognizes a deep interconnectivity between the success or sins of an individual and the whole community can trace its roots through the ancient Judeo-Christian mindset (Exod 12:1–16).

Thomas Merton did not shy away from advocating for moral change regarding immoral actions that were embedded and culturally accepted, such as institutional racism and violence, especially generated from war. In his essay, *Letter to an Innocent Bystander*, Merton stated that a societal bystander who complacently lives within a society of immoral norms and does not act for moral change cannot be considered innocent. He argued that the very lack of engagement to correct the moral wrong casts guilt on the complicit bystander.[26] This challenging perspective of Merton continues to serve as a prophetic reminder that advocates for change of socially accepted moral wrongs are essential in every society.

25. Daggy, "Thomas Merton & the Quiz Show Scandal," 10.
26. Merton, "Letter to an Innocent Bystander," 53–62.

Adolescents and Bullying:
Practical Application with Adolescents

As youth define their role in various micro-communities, children suffering from instabilities such as lacking a holistic perspective in the acknowledgment of their own dignity will often claim power by defining norms for that community, often through violent actions and responses. Individuals who become a threat to those claiming power, and establishing the community norms, are then labeled as other, and ridiculed, then ostracized. In his study of adolescent bullying, Michael Huggins indicated that the labeling and process of dehumanization cast upon the nonconformist within a community will develop into a stigma which then becomes the root and reason of the perpetuation of isolating and bullying behavior in the mind and actions of the aggressors. Merton summarizes it even more plainly:

> This terrible situation is the pattern and prototype of all sin: the deliberate and formal will to reject disinterested love for us for the purely arbitrary reason that we simply do not want it.[27]

Thomas Merton's call for peace and nonviolent resistance at its core is based on the keen awareness of the dignity of the human person. Throughout his writings on Christian Humanism, Merton explored the desire of the human person for teleological happiness;[28] such happiness is only found in the discovery of the authentic self created in union with God. For adolescents, this search for happiness is bound in the search for a full-embracing community, love. Bullying and isolation is bound in the rejection of the happiness of the *other*, as Merton stated.

Practical Examen: Questions for Reflection

- When have *I* purposefully rejected the love of another because *I* simply did not want it?

- Am *I* creating an atmosphere, especially around adolescents, that supports and encourages their search for happiness?

- Have *I* attempted to bridge or reconcile two groups, cliques, or ideological communities through prayer and patience?

27. Merton, *Seven Storey Mountain*, 26.
28. Merton, *Love and Living*, 135–232; Merton, *No Man Is an Island*, 127.

- Thomas Merton indicated that peace is necessary in one's self before affecting others, have *I* spend time exploring my needs to find inner peace?

- How have *I* created, invited, or allowed an adolescent to let down their mask and offer an opportunity for them to discuss real and tangible challenges in their life, without judgment or criticism?

- Have *I* offered support and an encouraging environment when an adolescent is being treated as a scapegoat or isolated from their peer group? How might Merton's words be used to remind us to strive for community instead of division?

13

Dialogue

The Ability to Communicate, Live, and Grow Together

The deepest level of communication is not communication, but communion. It is wordless. It is beyond speech, and it is beyond concept.[1]

IT IS IMPORTANT TO understand that Thomas Merton, although a man of numerous words and writings, experienced authentic dialogue through a transcendental nature; words and actions can still limit the deepest yearnings of the heart and soul. He believed that human language was only the starting point for communion. Much like prayer, words lay a foundation for a relationship with God but the words are only a vehicle for the intent of the actions. In the quote above, Merton reminds the reader that dialogue has much more to do with the depths of the human soul than the language utilized to give expression to that longing.

Dialogue lays the framework for relationship. Without the skills or ability to interpret the words, actions, or intent of others a healthy dialogue cannot be established. The contemporary technological culture, although creating new and faster forms for communication, has also placed limits upon that communication. To explore the exponential increase of how technology has changed communication opportunities compare the exponential evolution over the past two decades, where cultural expectations and

1. Merton, *Asian Journals*, 308

trends of adolescents have changed significantly. With the technological revolution of the twentieth century the face of communication, commerce, literacy, careers, education, and entertainment have changed exponentially.[2] One tangible example of such drastic change can be in found in the use of the Internet. The Internet expanded from using less than 1 percent of all information within telecommunications purposes to 97 percent, from 1993 to 2008.[3] Likewise, the development of popular applications like Twitter and Snapchat initially truncated the users abilities to communicate into very confined lengths; through the limited use of 140 characters[4] and a one-to-ten-second option for momentary viewing of photos, per application respectively. The purpose of this quick access was probably best described by Snapchat CEO, Evan Spiegel, in 2012: "Snapchat isn't about capturing the traditional Kodak moment. It's about communicating with the full range of human emotion—not just what appears to be pretty or perfect." This life-in-the-raw or life-on-the-go mentality has clearly made its mark on the technological age, based on the amount of users of such applications.[5] If dialogue is occurring more frequently but in more contained forms what does that mean for communication, as a whole?

Merton: On Communication as Living for Others

Thomas Merton was not a man of few words; and at times throughout his life identified himself primarily as a writer. In his book, *The Spiritual Genius of Thomas Merton*, Anthony Padovano recounted one particular experience where Merton was involved in a reaction-timed psychological test, where he was supposed to completed the sentence: "I am . . ." His reaction, in the moment, was "I am Thomas Merton the famous author."[6] Through this immediate reaction, Merton consciously or subconsciously recognized that his vocation was deeply bound by communicating with others. It

---

2. See: Carr, *The Shallows*; Greenfield, *Mind Change*; and Pacheco, *The Rise of the Human Digital Brain*.

3. Hilbert and Lopez, "The World's Technological Capacity to Store, Communicate, and Compute Information," 60–65.

4. Twitter later doubled the character limit to 280 in November 2017; while Snapchat expanded the viewing length of a picture to 24 hours in 2013.

5. As of February 2019, Twitter reported to have 321 million active users; while as of October 2019, Snapchat reported to have 210 million user a day.

6. Padovano, *The Spiritual Genius of Thomas Merton*, 37.

would be no exaggeration to agree with Merton's reaction. His communication through poetry, correspondence, and spiritual writing have become a legacy that perpetuates his thought and feelings beyond his death. Merton, the famous author, was much more than that, though; and as mentioned previously he wanted to be known as more than just a famous author. We all want to be remembered beyond the words of our conversations; there is more to each of us than just words on a page.

With a word of caution, I would like to remind the reader that Merton did not always remain this clear and direct throughout his writing. Reading his journals and letters, Merton shows the reader that he continued to struggle with finding the right way to communicate his feelings. He was not clear on how to express his frustration to his abbot, but writes about them in his journals, possibly expressing his deep-held convictions, or just venting some anger about the liturgies, Merton nonetheless concluded:

> I would say this and many other things, all adding up to one: our life here is a lie. If that is really the case, then, since I can't do anything about it, I had better leave. But always the question remains: perhaps it is I who am the liar and perhaps leaving would be the greater lie.[7]

Here we begin to understand the wisdom of Suzanne Zuercher as she reflected about Merton's personality and creative nature.

> When we listen to [The Individualist][8] speak about personal experience, we often hear philosophical summaries that sound disembodied and distant. Such summarizes in Merton's works are a product of grappling with inconsistencies he sees inseparable from living . . . Never be fooled, however. They, too, are raw reality honed into appropriate expression.[9]

While offering advice on writing and critical responses to one's art to Antoinette Costa, an adolescent, Merton honestly stated: "The whole question of communication is a very difficult one, and most difficult when one

---

7. Merton, *Journals of Thomas Merton*, 3:285.

8. The Individualist is a title for one of the personal types of the enneagram. The original quotation from Zuercher uses the number for the type, 4, instead of the title. A 4 refers to one of the nine type descriptions of the enneagram. The enneagram is a personality type test and descriptor. The type of 4 is described as the Individualist, who is dramatic, creative, expressive. The Enneagram Institute states that a 4's basic desire is to "find themselves and their significance (to create an identity)." See www.enneagraminstitute.com for further information.

9. Zuercher, *Merton: An Enneagram Profile*, 65–66.

writes imaginatively and symbolically as I do."[10] Merton recognized that the world was full of inconsistency, especially regarding works of art and literature, as well as the unique perspectives of the viewer's appreciation of a given piece of art or literature. He was also well aware that an adolescent would struggle with a similar challenge. It is clear that Merton's advice, based on personal dialogue and experience, was put into words that an adolescent would understand. Merton offered a foundational insight to help the young adolescent writer be authentic to her art, while honestly separating the piece of her self within the art from the judgment of those who do not understand or respect the gift of that piece of art.

Adolescents in contemporary culture continue to be torn with inconsistencies and paradoxes of expectation. Many adolescents experience a culture that immediately judges and condemns a comment or post at face value, but also says that an individual should aspire to any possibility for their future. Many children growing up in twentieth-century American culture were told and reinforced that they could become anything that they wanted to be; but in all actuality that expectation was really bound upon the cultural standards of the time. Throughout adolescence, navigating value-laden judgments becomes commonplace. From comments on social media to friend groups, adolescents are painfully aware of the consequences of a mistyped comment, a wrong posting, or the ridicule of liking or having a relationship with the wrong person. As mentioned in the previous chapter such behavior could then evolve into isolation and a social stigma, limiting their acceptance into a community.

Adolescence and Communication

Communication is an essential aspect of the adolescent experience. The evolution of social media has become a vehicle for an expansive network of communication. Software developers have not just expanded the ability to communicate and share messages within social media applications, but also the need to communicate has become an integral part of video games such as Fortnite and the Call of Duty series. The need for strategy and communication have drawn in adolescents to find friends based on web-only experience and communication. Words are exchanged consistently throughout the Internet. But if Merton is correct, words alone are not sufficient for the type of communication or dialogue that the human heart ultimately yearns for.

10. Merton, "Letter to Antoinette M. Costa, May 13, 1965," 335.

Authentic dialogue is an efficacious sign of its goal or purpose; namely, unity with the other. Merton stated: "words will become *sacred* signs. They will acquire the power to set apart certain elements of creation and make them holy."[11] Adolescents desire unity; to be accepted and become part of something sacred and meaningful. The exchange of words, actions, and time lay the foundation for that deeper connectivity. Shaffer and Gordon offered insights into the complexity of deeper meaning and complexity of dialogue, especially with adolescent girls.[12] Although words and phrases may be easily understood by adults, the meaning by the adolescent could be completely different than interpreted. A dialogue with an adolescent can easily become a game of patience and interpretation and breaking of codes, symbols, and double-meanings. Again, although adolescents possess a large vocabulary for dialogue, it does not necessarily mean that the words match the deeper truth of the vocabulary or that the sacred meaning was accurately conveyed. What needs to occur to establish order between such confusion and chaos, within the life of an adolescent and an adult?

11. Merton, *New Man*, 85.
12. Shaffer and Gordon, *Why Girls Talk and What They're Really Saying*, 3–20.

Dialogue: Through the Words
and Experiences of Adolescents

How can adolescents begin to heed the words of Thomas Merton? Through the thematic exploratory curriculum, based on Merton's writings, adolescents explored and experienced the theme of order. Merton stated that happiness was found through order, balance, rhythm, and harmony. Through the session focused on order in our lives, the students collaborated to experience and establish rules and structures, through the use of the game Jenga, to help create strategies to build and sustain a community.

While working in small groups, the adolescent students needed to develop ways to communicate effectively and engage with each other to learn from the experience by trying to keep their Jenga tower up as long as possible. Jenga is primarily known as a children's stacking block game, where individual blocks are removed from lower levels of the tower and placed at the top of the tower, creating a new row of three blocks; this process continues while the players try not to cause the tower of blocks to fall due to an imbalance created by the instability of lacking blocks on the lower rows of the tower. Throughout the course of the game, the tower of blocks will often become unstable, and will eventually fall.

In this activity the Jenga tower serves as a metaphor for the students regarding the need for order, through stability and wise communication. Involvement was demonstrated through playing Jenga, as a group, personal reflections on the open-ended questions, and a large group reflection of the activity.

The following narrative vignettes will illustrate as supporting evidence of aesthetic engagement by demonstrating sensory, logical, emotional, and ethical connections expressed by the students throughout the course of the implementation. The following sequential vignettes illustrate some of the engagement and dialogue shared within the experiences of the adolescents in the particular groups throughout the course of the group activity. I have included comments about student posture and movement to offer contextual support with the tone and expressions of the students that occurred during the activity:[13]

---

13. The following vignettes were all transcribed from the same group activity that took place on April 23, 2018.

Group 3

[Students sitting cross-legged around the tower, looking intently for the next best move] James [uses a pencil to test the movement of several of blocks to find a loose piece]

James [with excitement, gesturing at a side piece in the center of the tower]: Up here! Up here!

Harold [with passion]: DON'T TIP IT

James: [lays on the floor surrounding the tower with his arms and starts removing the piece; the tower starts to tip; the piece is removed safely]

Harold [relief; his hand covering his mouth]: ohh

James: [opens one of his hands perpendicular to the ground, in the "drop the mic" gesture; exuding pride]

Some of the students, such as James, decided to use creative measures, like the use of a pencil to help push blocks out of the row of the tower without shaking the structure. James also demonstrated his level of excitement when his creativity pays off, impressing his peers, and celebrating his individual victory. Other groups illustrated encouragement and more of a teamwork mentality.

Group 1

Brad [pointing out a block that is stuck; loud, nervous]: you can't put both hands on it

Brad [speaking to another student with enthusiasm]: you're doing good

Larry [congratulatory]: that's straight!

Brad [poking different blocks, finds a loose block on the edge, pushes it halfway out, and allows another student to remove the block]

Richard: [starts poking at the blocks trying to find a loose one]

Brad [excited—hand motioning to stop]: chill, chill

Richard: [gets a block halfway out]

Brad [anxious, passionate]: no that one, its gonna fall!

Richard: [pushes it back, tries to move it again]

Brad [with more excitement, desperate]: the top's gonna fall!

Richard: [gets the block out and puts it on top]

Brad [incredulously]: I have no clue, how on earth did that not fall?

Brad points at a block [nervous, loud]: if you take that one, it's gonna fall.

Group 5

Donald [suggesting]: this one looks loose

Timothy [nervous, trepidation]: wait

Robert [excited and encouraging]: do it! do it! do it!

Donald [removes the piece gently with precision, then relief]: whoo

Robert: [claps with approval]

Timothy [congratulatory]: Donald's got the skills!

Several of the students demonstrated verbal encouragement of others in their groups, as a good move occurred. Students also demonstrated their passion and began to be more animated as the game progressed and their tower became less stable. The adolescents would often offer advice on particular pieces to move, as an example of their group collaboration, as demonstrated in the previous narratives. As the game progressed further, and many of the towers became more unstable, the students become confused as to how to proceed; some groups, like Group 1, relied on dialoging with each other to work out a solution, while other groups, like Group 3, proceeded without caution or cooperation.

Group 1

Brad [confused]: alright what should we do?

Richard: [leans in slowly, starts moving a piece; tower sways]

Brad [cautious]: Hold on, Richard

Richard [looks confused, seeking advice]: what should we do?

Brad [flustered]: I don't know.

Group 3

[a block falls to the ground after being pushed]

Grady: [places the piece on top of the tower; the tower starts to lean but still stands]

Harold: whoo hoo! [laughs with confidence]

James: [leans in without consulting with the group; flicks a piece out of the bottom row]

[the tower falls; the students put their hands up to their heads in disgust]

Harold [in frustration]: OH NO

All students in the group together: JENGA!

The following day the students were given an opportunity to reflect on their experiences of the group activity in written responses and then in a large group discussion about the experience. Throughout these shared experiences the adolescents indicated that positive reinforcement, calm communication, and creative collaboration helped to establish an environment for successful strategy and group dynamics. In contrast, some of the students indicated that anger, resentment, and aggression create unhealthy atmospheres that lead to mistakes, lack of respect, and ultimately failure in the group task. While exploring the student experiences of successful aspects of group dynamics, the following experiences were mentioned.[14]

> Jerome [confidently]: your decisions affect everyone in the group, not just yourself.
>
> Larry [soft, timid]: um, we kind of were quiet and didn't get angry at each other, 'cause we knew that anger can make mistakes occur.
>
> Harold [matter-of-factly, with confidence]: well, we kept on, we like encouraged each other to keep the attitude positive because if we started being negative, um, putting each other down, we just fail quicker.
>
> Steve [anxiously]: well like, um, we just really didn't raise our voices or sound like we were trying to like make, make ourselves like the someone in charge. We kept it on like not being able to

---

14. The following vignettes were transcribed from a verbal class reflection and large group discussion on April 24, 2018, about the previous day's activity.

like, um, speak loudly or like make it so that we were sounding like not having acts of aggression, which would make other people, like, aggressive, like, towards, like calling out or like, like having it fall down. By doing that we were able to go peacefully forward.

Jerome [reflectively]: I felt the Jenga activity, uh, gave us perspective about foundation and how it's made and it illustrates a good example of like how like community nations and stuff have to be formed and it's all about order and if there is no order then it can crumble.

At the conclusion of the group discussion of the adolescent experiences of the collaborative game, I invited the students to concisely summarize their experiences. Several of the students consistently shared that there were good group dynamics that rely on including and consulting everyone in the group. Through their jotted notes of the activity, the students shared and explored further aspects of their experiences of beneficial group dynamics:[15]

Oakland [clearly, with a sigh]: things can go very poorly very quickly if we don't communicate with each other.

Matthew [cheerfully]: um, I would say that we need to, need to rely on each other to have success.

Steve [thinking-out-loud]: um, by looking at various safe alternative courses you can find the best option.

James [passionately]: everybody is an equal part of the group.

Although the comments stated above were not consistent among all of the adolescents, they nonetheless offer insight into student interpretations of the group activity experience and have peripheral connection with the emerging themes of the data, which will be explored in the following section:[16]

Grady: need to stay organized

Scotty: not being quick to blame that person if it fails

Jerome: people can't be greedy or selfish

15. The following vignettes were also transcribed from the large group discussion on April 24, 2018.

16. The following artifacts came from the students' written reflections about the same experience, collected on April 24, 2018.

Donald: know what the community needs

Oakland: remain calm and continue to strategy [sic] . . . listen to each other's insights

The emergent themes of this session and activity, based on the concept of order, were: the need for order, the need for healthy and clear communication, and that each individual has unique insights to contribute to the whole of the group. The students' data indicated that there was a recognition that order and structure have importance in society. Richard wrote: "order is important because you need to have structure in society and without any rules there would be choas [sic], and it would be a mess." Several students also indicated that clear communication is key for successful group dynamics. Oakland stated: "things can go poorly very quickly if we don't communicate well with others." Several students also indicated through their writings that each person has a unique and essential part to play within the whole. Matthew stated: "we need to rely on each other to have success."

Theologically, these themes connect with two core aspects of Catholic traditions: the term "apostolic," as referring to the mark of the church and Paul of Tarsus's body of Christ imagery, where everyone holds a unique and important part of the ministry of Jesus. The nature of the apostolic tradition, one of the four marks of the church, can be divided into two perspectives: the lineage, hierarchy, or succession of the apostles and evangelization.[17] Apostolic succession refers to the structure or order that developed from passing on the teaching authority from one bishop to the next, originating and bound to the spiritual lineage of the apostles. This sacred order is preserved to protect doctrine and establish and perpetuate the continuity of the teaching authority from the time of the apostles to the contemporary. This order maintains and protects the structure and authoritative nature of Catholic teaching throughout the centuries. While the second aspect of the apostolic mark of the church is an act of passing on the teachings and doctrine, evangelization. Throughout the adolescent reflections, there was a consistency in recognizing the need for systematic order and rules, while also being able to communicate and convey the rule or message well with others.

Secondly, the students consistently indicated that each person serves an important part of the community. Some of the adolescents remarked that "each person has an important role," "that it is important to learn insights

---

17. *Catechism of the Catholic Church*, §§77, 857.

for others," or "it is important to rely on each other for success." These concepts mirror Paul of Tarsus's theology of the recognition of the unique gifts and contributions each individual has for the church community, known as the body of Christ (Rom 12:5; 1 Cor 12:27). In Paul's perspective each person has a unique function and talent that aides the whole and, because of that individual calling, deserves respect within the whole community. Throughout the data, the student-participants stated that each individual may offer a new perspective or different outlook which may help to solve a problem with a beneficial new solution. In *Conjectures of a Guilty Bystander*, Merton also reflected on the very topic of order when he contrasts healthy order versus systematic indoctrination. He indicates that true order is found in and within the unique authenticity of the individual, through freedom and intelligence.

Practical Examen: Questions for Reflection

- Have *I* offered a patient response to the concerns or questions of an adolescent, or am *I* quick to say "no," challenge, or condemn an adolescent's idea(s)?

- Have *I* tried to communicate with adolescents through technological mediums that have importance and meaning for them, such as contemporary social media applications?

- Have *I* created opportunities for an adolescent to understand the importance of healthy communication with others?

- Do *I* communicate clearly and well with adolescents, or do *I* expect an adolescent to know the meaning behind my words?

- Have *I* been honest with an adolescent about family, work, or ministry expectations, as well as why those expectations are important for order within a community?

- Have *I* given an adolescent the opportunity to contribute their skills to develop leadership and/or opportunities to be proud of their contribution to a community?

14

Community

Establishing a Foundation for Authentic Relationship

He who attempts to act and do things for others or for the world without deepening his own self-understanding, freedom, integrity, and capacity to love, will not have anything to give others.[1]

FOR THOMAS MERTON, RELATIONSHIPS play an essential part of a whole and healthy human being. Merton did not retreat away from life in communion of others but found life-defining relationships inside and outside his monastic community. His chronicles of correspondence attest to the numerous meaningful relationships he had cultivated throughout his life.[2] He seemed to thrive especially on relationships that brought him into a deeper sense of his authentic self and vocation. From *Seven Storey Mountain* and throughout his journals and correspondence, Merton laid a blueprint of the importance of the individuals in his life, and offered insights as to their sacred presence on his own life and calling. Even though an individual may have only had a short period of time, chronologically, in his life their importance for Merton upon his lifelong identity was often profound. It is through such profundity that the heart of community is established.

1. Merton, "Contemplation in a World of Action," 375.
2. See Merton, *Life in Letters*; Merton, *Road to Joy*; and Merton, *Witness to Freedom*.

Much like Merton, adolescents find worth and value through defining relationships. As mentioned previously, adolescents seek out peer groups with common interests and desire acceptance and to be understood. Contemporary youth have found new and evolving avenues to find and define relationships and peer groups beyond traditional forms of athletics, extracurricular clubs, and friend groups; through social media groups, online gaming platforms, and virtual spaces which are still in the process of evolving. Instead of tangible realities, and one-to-one personal relationships that develop into deep communities of persons, adolescents today often find relationships in virtual space more convenient than in tangible proximity. No matter the nature of the environment, though, the concept of community and interconnectivity is present in the life of an adolescent.

The Human Longing for Community

The desire to be part of a community is a deep longing in the nature of the human person. Even though athletics place great pride in honors like a MVP, or Hall of Fame inductee, the honored star will always recognize those individuals who were instrumental in the life of that athlete and challenged him or her to strive for more in a speech of gratitude. The same is true for speeches given at film awards, music awards, and even great artists who find a muse to inspire timeless art. The human condition is one of being part of a larger and inspirational community. Great novels and dramatic stories offer the same insight—take the examples of classics like *Little Women* and *Anne of Green Gables*. The stories are just as much about the main and independent character as those around that character who support and influence their development. In the action genre, the Harry Potter series, Star Wars, and the Marvel Universe, although focused on heroes and heroines, the success of the main protagonists is dependent on the assistance of and collaboration with others for victory.

Some of the greatest novel examples of this need and dependence for community in holistic maturation would be the *Chronicles of Narnia*, *The Hobbit*, and *The Lord of the Rings* stories. Both C. S. Lewis and J. R. R. Tolkien, respectively, developed stories that were specifically framed on a reliance on others, especially to defeat temptation or evil. This thematic plotline was not an accident, of course, as the very nature of the Christian message is based on the nature of community, and purposefully paralleled the life of Jesus and the apostles; or at the deepest core of belief the very nature of the Triune God. Catholic teaching states: "that the Son of God assumed a human nature in order to accomplish our salvation in it" and thus make humanity partakers in the divine nature.[3] Secular stories have mirrored this relationship through characters like the Lone Ranger and Tonto, Sherlock Holmes and Dr. Watson, and even the dynamic duo Batman and Robin.

Merton was well aware of the deep connection of humanity and God, through the sacred nature of the incarnation. Merton stated:

> I have the immense joy of being *man*, a member of a race in which God Himself became incarnate. As if the sorrows and stupidities of the human condition could overwhelm me, now I realize what we all are. And if only everybody could realize this! . . . Then it was as if I suddenly saw the secret beauty of their hearts, the depths of their hearts where neither sun nor desire nor self-knowledge can reach, the core of their reality, the person that each one is in God's eyes. If only they could see each other that way all the time.[4]

This epiphany experienced by Merton at the cross streets of 4th and Walnut, in downtown Louisville, offered a profound insight into the dignity and deep connective reality of humanity. This moment of enlightenment struck him to the core regarding his knowledge of the essence of human life as well as God's overflowing grace in the lives blessed through the incarnation. The transcendent experience, once and for all, made Merton painfully aware of the inadequacies of the physical human senses. This divine spark of connectivity to all of humanity became a catalyst for Merton's cry for advocacy of the divine reality of unity that exists at the heart of community.

Merton: Insight into the Need for Community

Since his youth Merton longed for community. Although orphaned at sixteen, Merton yearned for a sense of connectivity to something more than his individuality. This draw toward community was initially satisfied through his friendships at Columbia but continued to deepen and grow beyond that small group of friends and mentors. This desire for community brought Merton's search into monastic life, with the Cistercians, but even that did not satisfy his longing for community, as he often searched to be moved or transferred to

3. *Catechism of the Catholic Church*, §§ 460–61.
4. Merton, *Conjectures of a Guilty Bystander*, 154–55.

another community.[5] Even later in life, he felt drawn to pursue a relationship with M. to the point of questioning his commitment and monastic vows, but even that did not satisfy his desire for community. Ultimately, he felt drawn to the East and an ecumenical desire to find community with other monastic traditions. Would that have fulfilled his longing for community? Who knows? Some individuals were convinced that Merton did not intend to return from the East; while others believed that he would never have been able to leave Gethsemani. What is known is that Thomas Merton yearned for community. He yearned to be accepted as an authentic individual, searching from earth to the heavens to find community.

LITANY

All holy souls
    pray for us fellows,
all Carmelites pray
all Third Orders,
all sodalities,
    all altar societies,
all action groups,
all inaction groups,
all beat up shut in groups,

5. See Lipsey, *Make Peace Before the Sun Goes Down*; as well as Grayston, *Thomas Merton and the Noonday Demon*.

all without money groups,
pray for the rich Trappist cheese groups
vice versa
mutual help,
　　amen, amen.[6]

This prayer-poem shows the inherent connectivity between all sorts of groups and people in fellowship with the divine. Although this is only one example of the many poetic prayers Merton entitled "Litany,"[7] he shows the inclusion of various in-groups and out-groups through the use of opposites of similar grouping identities.

Adolescence and Communities

Seeking, searching, and becoming part of a community is an inherent aspect of adolescence. Throughout this stage of life, teens are in the search for their role in society, acceptance in and through relationships, and ultimately their authentic self. Adolescence bridges a gap between innocence and maturity, and is a time defined by discovery, acceptance in relationships, and communities apart from their family; a time of emancipation from the bounds of childhood to a more self-determined adulthood. Through the ability to experiment with community experiences that differ from their family and familiar expectations, an adolescent comes to learn their unique calling and personal preferences in relationship with others.

This youthful vigor, adolescence, is a stage of life full of holistic growth, struggle, change, and passion.[8] Throughout this stage of growth and search for independence, from the parental definitions and confines associated with youthfulness, adolescents yearn for self-identity and community. Adolescents also search for authentic self-development, based on direct or indirect inclusion within other peer groups. This desire for identity can often create discord with previously held traditions or beliefs that have been instilled in them by their parents or figures in authoritative roles as they try to find their place in the world. While coming of age, adolescents test their previous creeds and codes in search for their own views of the world, negotiating between the past and present to engage their future.

---

6. Merton, "Litany," 724–25.

7. See Merton, *Collected Poems of Thomas Merton*, 724–26.

8. See Marcia et al., *Ego Identity*.

Throughout the walls of a high school one will quickly see the various communities comprised of adolescents that come together through similar interests. These adolescent communities are often stereotyped in television and film, such as through the examples of the group of nerds and geeks in television shows like *Freaks and Geeks* (1999–2000) or films like *Galaxy Quest* (1999), musical and glee clubs as in the hit television show *Glee* (2009–15), and even harsher and more judgmental adolescent communities as illustrated in *Mean Girls* (2004). In the midst of such labeled and community identities, adolescents are in the process of merely searching for inclusion and acceptance. Scholars on adolescent development, within the context of secondary school environments, have indicated that relationships have fundamental importance for this age.[9]

Community: Through the Words and Experiences of Adolescents

Throughout this manuscript we have discussed themes that connect adolescent spiritual with the life and writings of Thomas Merton. If adolescent spirituality scholars are correct and adolescents gravitate toward a Moral Therapeutic Deist perspective, they will be missing a holistic perspective of relationship with God. As helpful as the NSYR data has been, there still remain many questions about adolescent spirituality that need further investigation. To what extend is there is a sense of entitlement and indifference in American culture at large? To what degree is there a complete view of the struggles, sufferings, and sacrifices of life in the media influence of youth and young adults in American culture? How much more powerful is the media culture's message of life and happiness compared to a Christian parent's view on their children? To what degree is an average adult or youth able to articulate their faith when questioned? Even with such remaining questions adolescent spirituality scholars Arthur Canales and Kenda Creasy Dean have stated that it is important for adolescents to have the opportunity to reflect on experiences with others, such as service-learning opportunities, through a real-life context and with language that can help them articulate and claim their own experiences. To have a tangible experience of community many schools and youth ministry programs include

9. Brandy Quinn's article "Purposeful Explorers" examined that some contemporary researchers have suggested that twenty-first-century Catholic educators should adopt relationship-building skills within the framework for Catholic high school curriculums.

a service component with their yearly curriculum. Such service opportunities allow adolescents to be present and actively find harmony with the challenges and needs of their local community.

Based on the four themes Merton defined as the path to happiness in *No Man Is an Island*, namely order, balance, rhythm, and harmony, the theme of harmony was explored in the exploratory curriculum using the documentary film, *The Human Experience*, to serve as a bridge to help the students explore their own experiences regarding their community service projects during their school year. Evidence of student engagement and involvement with the curriculum was demonstrated through watching the film, jotting notes and reflecting on it, as well as through small group and large group discussions. The following narrative vignettes serve as supporting evidence of aesthetic engagement by demonstrating sensory, logical, emotional, and ethical connections expressed by the students throughout the course of the implementation.

After watching the documentary, the students were given fifteen minutes to discuss open-ended questions in small groups, consisting of three or four students, before they assembled into a large circle for a larger class dialogue.[10] The first question was for the students to define the term "harmony" in their own words.

Harold: harmony—a balance of peace and togetherness

Richard: harmony—working together as one

Robert: harmony—working together in unison, peace

Donald: harmony—being at peace in your life, happy, working together in unison

The written responses for this part of the activity were composed primarily of very static answers that focused on the face-value perspective of the term. When the adolescents begun to verbally share their thoughts, the definitions became to develop further.[11]

Jerome [timidly]: it's uh, like a balance, like, between a community; kind of where it's kind of stable.

10. The following artifacts came from the students' written reflections, collected on April 17, 2018.

11. The following vignettes came from transcriptions of the students' verbal reflections during a class dialogue on April 17, 2018.

Timothy [speaking, while thinking out loud]: it's where people are all just working together as well, and just, they work together to finish a task.

Oakland [with confidence]: I think harmony is being able to interact with a person, communicate with them, be able to understand them on a more personal level than just what you see—try to go to their past and understand them.

There was consistency present in the written and verbally shared reflections that highlighted the students' interpretations of definitions for the term harmony. The student definitions included a relationship with others on a deep holistic level, united in the same *telos* or goal, and a sense of being at peace within the relationship or community. As the students became more comfortable and confident in the atmosphere of the large circle their responses were more articulate and defined and offered a willingness to explore new beliefs and change from previous ideologies which illustrated disequilibrium in their thought processes. A similar contrast was present between the written and verbal responses for the definition of the term " discord."[12] Consider the following responses which illustrate the students' exploration and shared interpretative experiences of discord:

Richard [written response]: working independently and not rhythmically

Robert [written response]: opposite of harmony, out of control, choas [*sic*]

Donald [written response]: something is wrong with your life, unhappy, arguments

Harold: [verbal response; started soft and timidly but ended louder with more confidence]: it's like, you'll probably have discord when you can't, like, you don't understand another person; like two different religions will normally have discord because they're not understanding each other, most of the time they're not even trying to.

Oakland [verbal response; clear, without hesitation]: I think discord is stereotyping or having a misunderstanding of a person just based off what they've done.

12. The following artifacts came from the students' written reflections and transcriptions from the class dialogue, collected on April 17, 2018.

The student responses above illustrate that the students consistently interpreted discord as a negative experience; one student even used the example of two different religions unable to dialogue as an example of discord. When the student-participants were prompted to explore what is needed when discord is present in a community or environment, one student led the conversation:[13]

> Jerome [verbal response; soft volume but with passion]: my advice is to find common ground; like something you both agree upon.

As the dialogue evolved the adolescents became more comfortable in the circle of their peers and began to share and explore the common-ground experiences they had in their community-service project experiences. The conversation naturally evolved beyond the context of the film as a frame of reference and exploring their own personal community service experiences:

> Harold [normal volume with enthusiasm, proud of his work]: well I volunteer at the children's hospital downtown and we like to volunteer to, like, check on the patients to see how they're doing and like bring them stuff when they need it, and we'll play with some of the kids there and just try to make their day better. So, that what I did.

> Steve [soft volume but with passion]: I worked at a [local family homeless shelter name #1] Christmas party with the wrestling team and we got them presents and like, just played around with them for about an hour.

> Jerome [normal volume, casual, but later surprised while remembering the experience]: I went to [local homeless shelter name #2], uh, homeless shelter for men with the soccer team and so we went and talked to the homeless people, and had to serve them lunch . . . It brought me closer to people who I never would have never spent time with outside of service. We were there and not distracted. I learned, how like, that even if they don't have what I have they still make the best of it and have fun. Well, so, like when you're on a team, a big part of it is chemistry—sit down and talk as a team.

> Larry [verbal response; normal volume but collecting his thoughts]: um, I went with the lacrosse team to a Walmart, out, um, I forgot where it was, but we did shopping with kids with, uh, less fortunate, their families were on less fortunate times so that

13. The following vignettes came from transcriptions of the students' verbal reflections during a class dialogue on April 17, 2018.

they could have new clothes, and like winter coats, and a couple of toys for like the Christmas season. Uh, I established common ground by talking with them about, like, what sports they like to play and through what clothes they wear. If they liked a lot of toys and stuff, like if they wanted footballs and stuff. I would talk about, like, playing football or if they'd like to play like board games, or video games, I would talk about video games.

This concept of establishing common ground with others parallels the Catholic Church's perspective of ecumenical understanding of building bridges and creating a dialogue on similar beliefs instead of isolating others by focusing on their different beliefs or ideologies.[14] Merton scholar John Moses argued that ecumenism, at its roots of universality or finding common ground, was what Thomas Merton believed was at the very core of the nature of the Catholic Church.[15] The later works of Thomas Merton particularly focused on interreligious dialogue to bridge Western and Eastern spirituality, beyond abstract institutional theory but true contact on a holistic individual human level. This concept of ecumenism is not formally introduced within the USCCB framework until second semester of sophomore year and then explored more thoroughly junior year within the social justice course, as well as in the senior year in the world religions course.[16] Merton believed that this type of connection and recognition helps humanity recognize the sacred in the other, especially individuals who are usually labeled as outcasts (e.g., homeless, sick . . .).[17] The following adolescent responses illustrate the sacred nature of the other, who are labeled as outcasts in society:[18]

> Timothy [soft volume, a bit hesitant in his response]: I learned that homeless people are the same as us, they just don't have a home. They are very friendly and welcoming.

> Oakland [normal volume, confident]: I learned that everyone has a story. We sometimes forget that someone has experiences that have worth. We forget that these people are from a different place and that has different views based off.

14. *Catechism of the Catholic Church*, §816.

15. See Moses, *Divine Discontent*.

16. See *Doctrinal Elements of a Curriculum*.

17. See Merton, *Conjectures of a Guilty Bystander*.

18. The following artifacts came from the students' written reflections and transcriptions from the class dialogue, collected on April 17, 2018.

Jerome [normal volume, a little anxious—like he's trying to figure out what he wants to say]: everybody's good, everybody's the same, it's just how you experience the world.

Harold [written response]: They [the actors in the film] treated them [individuals with leprosy] with dignity and respect b/c [sic] it's what all humans deserve.

As indicated here, the theme of recognizing the dignity and worth of the other clearly emerged from the verbal and written student responses. The written and verbal conversation presented here illustrate that the students were interpreting, from the experiences of the film and their own experiences, that human dignity is something greater than the labels or isolating stigma placed upon others, especially individuals who are stereotyped because of poverty or chronic health conditions.

Theologically, two themes directly correspond to two core aspects of Catholic doctrine: ecumenism and interfaith dialogue, and the dignity of the human person. These two concepts are greatly revered in the Catholic Constitutional documents of Vatican II in *Sacrosanctum Concilium* and *Gaudium et Spes*, as well as the most current catechetical resources from the USCCB.[19] Although the students did not specifically read the writings of Thomas Merton for this topic the adolescents were able to articulate, through their language and experiences, concepts that consistently resonate with the spirit of interfaith dialogue and the dignity of the human person that permeate throughout Merton's Christian Humanist perspective and writings. If I were to include Merton's writing in another iteration of the exploratory curriculum I would have adolescents read sections on Merton's epiphany experience at Fourth and Walnut, as well as his letter to Besti Baeten and correspondence selections from *Witness to Freedom*, and several selections of his poetry of social advocacy, to help adolescents engage with the realities of Merton's experience and its insights for issues within our contemporary communities.

Practical Examen: Questions for Reflection

- Have *I* actively tried to build relationship and spiritual communion with adolescents?

19. See "Living as Missionary Disciples."

- Have *I* actively dialogued with an adolescent about their beliefs and why such beliefs are important in their life?

- Have *I* created opportunities for an adolescent to understand the importance of community, family, and the church?

- Do *I* actively witness a communal spirit with those around me, especially adolescents?

- Have *I* explored the difference between respected aspects of community life through secular examples in comparison to the church?

- Have *I* engaged in ecumenism or interreligious dialogue to become a witness of community and collaboration within the global nature of the twenty-first century?

15

The World

Becoming One with the Known and Unknown

Into this world, this demented inn, in which there is absolutely no room for
Him at all, Christ has come uninvited. But because He cannot be at home in it,
because He is out of place in it, and yet He must be in it, His place is with those
others for whom there is no room.[1]

THROUGH THIS ADVENT REFLECTION, Thomas Merton starkly contrasts
a world open to Christ and one that is not. He poetically connects our
contemporary trajectory of the world with the nature of the region that
Joseph and Mary sought refuge in during the census, before the birth of
Jesus. Merton plainly stated here that Christ came for the rejected, outcast, and individuals who society did not have room for; a people of his
own. What are we actually becoming part of through maturation? What
type of world are we contributing to? Merton's words continue to raise a
challenge that the need to be open to Christ, to have room in the inn, not
only is an individual responsibility but is also a communal responsibility. We must witness healthy lifestyles and spiritual insights for the next
generation to follow and learn from.

To address the spiritual needs of contemporary adolescents it is important to recognize that they have only known a world based on wireless

---

1. Merton, "Time of the End Is the Time of No Room," 72.

communication. This generation of adolescents commonly uses text messaging more frequently than telephone calls and often finds and defines relationships based on social networking applications such as Snapchat, Twitter, or Instagram. Many adolescent social media users now judge their worth and popularity based on the amount of online friends, likes, and comments they receive from a particular posting.[2] These metrics have become the standard measure for credibility, social status, and inclusion for certain peer groups. With such heavy weight placed upon the judgment of metrics some scholars warn that such trends are developing narcissistic tendencies in this generation of youth and promote lack of engagement from real-life which can lead to addictive tendencies to virtual environments.[3]

Adolescents and the World

> The greatest need of our time is to clean out the enormous mass of mental and emotional rubbish that clutters our minds and makes all political and social life a mass illness. Without housecleaning we cannot begin to see. Unless we see, we cannot think. The purification must begin with the mass media. How?[4]

As established previously, to engage and thrive in a twenty-first-century environment adolescents need to develop skills in digital literacy, to help navigate and interpret their world. The field of research of how the digital universe has influenced change in the brain of youth, efficiency in student knowledge and productivity, and how such changes have affected education and spiritual formation have been growing in prominence for the last decade.[5] The digital world has affected students beyond knowledge acquisition and biology; it has also had affects on the moral behaviors, self-reflection, and personal reasoning skills of students. The moral implications of digital development are an aspect not often discussed in current ministry research. This text hopes to raise awareness of the need of the inclusion of moral implications in the discussion of digital literacy and the

---

2. Tosun, "Motives for Facebook Use and Expressing 'True Self' on the Internet," 1510–17.

3. Rosen, "Virtual Friendship and the New Narcissism," 172–88.

4. Merton, *Conjectures of a Guilty Bystander*, 64.

5. See Greenfield, *Mind Change*, and Pacheco, *Rise of the Human Digital Brain*.

consequences that can develop from the lack of moral thought in digital pedagogical conversations.

Through reading current news reports and watching popular sitcoms it is apparent that there is a need of a conversation of moral digital literacy. Throughout the US Presidential Election of 2016, there was a barrage of media stories alleging scandals from both major parties, which commentators, on both sides of the political spectrum, stated were not newsworthy but were fake news. Scholars on media industry and its influence Patrick Kennedy and Andrea Prat offered insight into the power of access to global communications and the effect of fake news on digital readers.[6] Fake news is a topic that will affect youth as they mature and engage current events in local and national scenes, but a topic directly relevant to the demographic of a youth and adolescent audience is the influence of media in sitcom. As previously mentioned, popular Netflix series *13 Reasons Why* also ignited a fierce debate about the judgment and degree of influence entertainment can have on the decisions and actions of adolescents. Research indicated that digital searches on adolescent suicide and suicidal ideation rose considerably after the release of the first season of the show.[7] How could moral decision-making in digital literacy help adults navigate between fake news and real news content? How could digital literacy assist adolescents and youth better navigate moral choices grounded in reality rather than seek to mimic the actions of fictional characters?

Although this text was influenced by educational experiences in an urban Catholic secondary school setting, that should not limit the conversation of moral behavior and application of moral judgment skills in digital literacy to be only acceptable in the private educational sphere. Educational pedagogical practices and ministry for adolescents should focus toward moral behaviors in both the private and secular sectors, especially in democratic societies where it can help students mature and engage in finding their authentic voice and contributing to topics affecting human dignity in their communities, such as movements of tolerance and collaborative-orientated respect of others. Elliot Eisner argued that curriculum goals should not focus on a particular set of reductionist skills but rather on expansive skills to assist students navigate their unpredicted future challenges, such as through skills of judgment, critical thinking, meaningful

6. Kennedy and Prat, "Where Do People Get Their News?," 17–65.

7. See Ayers et al., "Internet Searches for Suicide Following the Release of 13 Reasons Why."

literacy, collaboration, and service.[8] A moral sense of respect of one's self and of others is a necessary overarching skill needed in the twenty-first century world, and offers a new lens throughout which digital literacy can help a student holistically mature.

Merton: Union with Divine

At first sight it may have seemed anachronistic to explore and apply the writings of Thomas Merton to the concept of adolescent spirituality. It is impor-

tant to remember that Merton's thoughts and writings continue to offer insights into aspects of the topic of broader spirituality well ahead of his time. It is also important to acknowledge that Thomas Merton had a great division in his literature that contrasts the ascetic and monastic youthful convert, and the radical, creative activist, which can be a challenge when initially approaching the writings of Thomas Merton.[9] But coincidentally, the breadth of Merton's writings evolved much like an adolescent maturing from a youthful vigor to the patient wisdom of adulthood. Here, pictured with a goofy grin, Merton embodies the playful and engaging joy of an authentic relationship with God.

> This is what it means to seek God perfectly: to withdraw from illusion and pleasure, from worldly anxieties and desires, from the works that God does not want, from a glory that is only human in display; to keep my mind free from confusion in order that my liberty may be always at the disposal of His will . . . to gather all

8. Eisner, "Preparing for Today and Tomorrow," 6–10.

9. Shannon, *Thomas Merton: An Introduction*, 124.

that I am, and have all that I can possibly suffer or do or be, and abandon them all to God in the resignation of a perfect love and blind faith and pure trust in God, to do His will.[10]

Adolescents: Engaging the World in their Words

The themes of the following vignettes from the student journals do not neatly fall under the previous thematic sections mentioned in the previous themes of order, balance, rhythm, or harmony but are nonetheless an important aspect of witness to the experiences of adolescents' engagement of the world, through their interpretations of the explorative curriculum.[11]

> James: I started to think, is my voice ever going to be one that will cause change or will I just liveout [sic] my life not making any contribution. I don't want that to happen, I want to do something to make people know who I am. I want to do it in a good way though. I don't want to be the person that people warn others about. I want to make the world a better place… I want people to be less worried about their individual achievement and more on everyones [sic].

This student shared in his journaling that he felt challenged to think deeply about his life choices and his future legacy. NSYR scholars Christian Smith and Melinda Lundquist Denton as well as Kenda Creasy Dean indicated that adolescents have a desire for advocacy and self-discovery, which are clearly illustrated in these remarks.[12] For this student, these topics have also challenged him to move from a state of complacency to one of disequilibrium and reflection.

> Robert: I really liked the watching the film [*The Human Experience*]. It opened a window to something I have never experienced [sic]. I have never seen so much poverty, but out of that poverty was happiness. People with so little are happier than the people in America who have so much. This made me question my own happiness because I have so much but I am not as happy. This video showed me a new definition of happiness. I learned it isn't about physical property and owning a lot of stuff, but happiness is the relationships you make with other people.

10. Merton, *New Seeds of Contemplation*, 45–46.

11. The following artifacts came from the students' personal journal reflections based on the entire curriculum experience, collected on April 20, 2018.

12. See Dean, *Almost Christian*; and Smith and Denton, *Soul Searching*.

Similarly, this student acknowledged that the film moved his view from complacency to disequilibrium and reflection. This student also acknowledged that the experience of the curriculum material challenged him to reinterpret his definition of happiness. He stated that happiness is found in relationships with others which echoes the writings of Thomas Merton.[13]

> Steve: The Human Experience was eye opening for me. I felt very changed after seeing the film. I felt some of the things that people feel while going through their daily lives. The Idea [*sic*] that everyone has obsticles [*sic*] in their life is very strange in a way that now I cannot think of any person in a stereotypical way just because of what they have or are a part of. This is looking at both good and bad things. The Idea [*sic*] that when all you have is lost, but you are still fighting because they believe that God has a plan for them in the future.

This student indicated that the film *The Human Experience* moved his view from complacency, as well. This student also indicated that this perspective has changed his focus beyond labels and stereotypes but on an authentic dignity of the human person.

> Matthew: Another experience I enjoyed was watching The Human Experience. It was empowering to me. These 2 brothers really went for it. I want to go for it like that and make a major change in the process. Through my going for it, I want to make a difference in our world. The difference is something I can be proud of. All it takes is one step, one decision, to permenantly [*sic*] move forward in a fantastic, new, and electrifying direction. That's what I'm going to do—> TAKE the FIRST STEP to something great and powerful and freeing. Let's DO this!

This student's journal reflection does not focus on his change of perspective of others, but a renewed belief in himself. Although abstract the dialogue here contains great emotion and determination to make a change in his life and advocate for himself. This type of language mirrors the progression from complacency through disequilibrium to change. Through the use of dynamic writings, such as the capitalization and punctuation, this student illustrated a move in his mindset from consistency to disequilibrium, and to systematic change.

> Larry: Watching the film, The Human Experience, was a very opening experience. It has really expanded my view of the world,

13. See Merton, *No Man Is an Island*.

and it has provided me with many positive messages. The first message that comes to mind is that physical possessions don't really provide true happiness . . . Another message is that community is important . . . The last message that I took from the film was that you should always try to improve.

This student's journal writing combines many of the previous shared experiences of change of the definition of happiness and improving one's life.

Jerome: The circle [Socratic dialogue] was a fun thing to experience too. Even though some people didn't contribute, I got to hear how some of my classmates feel and also some things about them. I felt free to share my thoughts, and I never felt judged. Sometimes I feel like creating a circle of people makes me feel better than sitting in rows and columns.

This student's response indicates the importance he places on community and feeling connected with his peers. He interpreted the circle of his peers to be free, safe and nonjudgmental.

Throughout the course of the curriculum implementation four overarching themes emerged from the student-participants' data: all humanity has worth and value, it is essential to develop common ground with others, peace and calm are better than aggression and anger, and happiness is greater than material possessions.

All Humanity Has Worth and Value

Throughout the course of the curriculum implementation this theme was the most consistently present and shared throughout the student-participants' responses. This theme was shared by the students in various ways from directly mentioning that humanity has worth to stating that everyone has an important part within the whole community, or that everyone has their own story or experience.

During the session on harmony, students interpreted from the film and their service experiences that individuals outcasted because of poverty or sickness are not different than anyone else, as Jerome clearly summarized: "everyone's good, everybody's the same." Throughout the session on balance students recognized their own worth and need to take care of their health and wholeness. Steve stated: "from this I believe that I must take more time to analyze my own thoughts to alleviate some of the stress that I have." Oakland also reflected: "you need to step back and kind of figure out what you need to do to be your best self and figure if I'm doing something wrong and it so how do I fix it?" During the session on order, several students shared that each person offers an important part of the group. James stated: "everybody is an equal part of the group." Finally, during the session on rhythm there was consistent interpretations that everyone adds to the group. Harold summarized: "everyone is dependent on one another, and to me that is the definition of community."

It Is Essential to Develop Common Ground with Others

Throughout the course of the curriculum implementation, the concept of common ground was also a consistently prominent theme shared by the student-participants' responses. This theme was shared by the students from directly mentioning establishing common ground to know others on a deeper level than face value to understanding and having healthy communication to sustain order and rhythm. In conjunction with the previous overarching theme of recognizing the dignity of others, in this theme the students recognized a tactic to develop a relationship with others, in response to the isolation and alienation that often exists in cliches and bullying situations.

The concept of establishing common ground within relationships originated from Jerome: "my advice is to find common ground; like something you both agree upon." This theme then was then developed and explored by all the students through the remainder of the curriculum implementation. The students interpreted that it is through common ground that deep meaningful relationships with others are developed and sustained, by authentic sharing and listening to understand the other. Scotty stated: "This is understanding, when it is your turn to engage in the discussion and when it is your turn to sit back and listen to the other collaborators." Oakland also stated: "it is important to communicate with others."

Peace and Calm Are Better than Aggression and Anger

This overarching theme was shared by the students in various ways as well; from the direct experience of trying to stay calm within the midst of the stress of the group activity, the Jenga game, as well as the personal stresses (e.g. homework, family expectations, and sports) that affected the students. Many of the students did not realize the effect of such stresses until they were able to reflect on their experience of the stillness during the silent meditation. Several students interpreted that aggression and anger lead to mistakes and failures in group dynamics. Throughout the session on balance students consistently indicated that stress and anxiety weigh down their lives. During the topic on harmony, Scotty wrote that community is found through "working together in peace and harmony." Oakland mentioned similar insights in his reflections of the topic of balance: "I would like to meditate in the future. It would help me get out of my daily routine and find some peace and balance." During the conversation after the Jenga group activity, Larry indicated: "we kind of were quiet and didn't get angry at each other 'cause we knew that anger can make mistakes to occur." Donald also similarly reflected in his writings on the topic of rhythm: "I believe that rhythm can help someone become in tune in life because rhythm can make life tranquill [sic]."

Happiness Is Greater than Material Possessions

The overarching theme of happiness being greater than material possessions was also found throughout the course of the curriculum, although it was most consistently mentioned within the student reflections about the film and service experiences. Harold expressed his amazement when describing the life of community of lepers shown in *The Human Experience*: "they still went on with their lives even if they were in a bad situation they were still happy . . . and I thought that was really cool to see that." In his journal Robert wrote: "I learned it isn't about physical property and owning a lot of stuff, but happiness is the relationships you make with other people." Grady indicates a similar insight when describing the difference between the pressure of athletic goals and settling one's self in meditation: "my soccer tournament is causing me a lot of stress because there may be colleges watching me. School in general causing me stress because . . . I need to make sure I keep my grades up; I would like to meditate again in the future. It helped me feel very calm and relaxed. It was a nice change of pace." During his reflections on order Matthew reflected that order could lead to happiness: "Yes . . . order allows for positive things to grow." This theme seemed to be the most surprising as the students reflected in their writings and dialogues.

Using the writings and life of Thomas Merton as a lens, we can see that themes from these writings can apply and parallel many trends within the adolescent stage of life. Merton's honest, transparent, and authentic writing continues to have the ability to help adolescents who are searching for a mentor and guide through life's ups and downs, navigate the challenges of the world, and mature in faith to love the God and God's presence throughout the world. May we too follow in the witness and trust, as Thomas Merton did, in God's providence to not close our hearts as we become part of the Known and Unknown throughout the challenging but joy-filled ministerial journey with adolescents.

My Lord God, I have no idea where I am going. I do not see the road ahead of me. I cannot know for certain where it will end. Nor do I really know myself, and the fact that I think that I am following your will does not mean that I am actually doing so. But I believe that the desire to please you does in fact please you. And I hope I have that desire in all that I am doing. I hope that I will never do anything apart from that desire. And I know that if I do this you will lead me by the right road though I may know nothing about it. Therefore will I trust you always though I may seem to be lost and in the shadow of death. I will not fear, for you are ever with me, and you will never leave me to face my perils alone.[14]

14. Merton, *Thoughts in Solitude*, 83.

Bibliography

Abegg, Jimmy. *Ragamuffin Prayers*. Eugene, OR: Harvest, 2000.

Abeles, Vicki, and Grace Rubenstein. *Beyond Measure: Rescuing an Overscheduled, Overtested, Underestimated Generation*. New York: Simon & Schuster, 2015.

Abeles, Vicki, and Jessica Congdon, dirs. *Race to Nowhere: The Dark Side of America's Achievement Culture*. Lafayette, CA: Reel Link Films, 2009.

Adams, Ian. "The Lonely Death of Chanie Wenjack." *Maclean's*, February 1, 1967. https://www.macleans.ca/society/the-lonely-death-of-chanie-wenjack/.

Alter, Charlotte, et al. "TIME 2019 Person of the Year: Greta Thunberg." *TIME*, 2019. https://time.com/person-of-the-year-2019-greta-thunberg/.

Atkinson, Morgan C., dir. *The Many Stories and Last Days of Thomas Merton*. United States: Duckworks, 2015.

Augustine. *The Confessions*. Translated by Maria Boulding. New York: Vintage, 1998.

Ayers, John W., et al. "Internet Searches for Suicide Following the Release of 13 Reasons Why." *JAMA Internal Medicine* 177.10 (2017) 1527–29. https://jamanetwork.com/journals/jamainternalmedicine/fullarticle/2646773.

Baez, Joan. "Joan Baez." In *Merton: By Those Who Knew Him Best*, edited by Paul Wilkes, 416. New York: Harper & Row, 1984.

Barron, Bishop Robert. "Bishop Barron on 'Doctor Strange.'" *YouTube*, December 1, 2016. https://www.youtube.com/watch?v=_jewe-MqoTo.

———. "Bishop Barron on 'Why I Hate Religion, But Love Jesus.'" *YouTube*, January 18, 2012. https://www.youtube.com/watch?v=TLta2b9zQ64&vl=en.

Beauvois, Xavier, dir. *Of Gods and Men*. France: Why Not Productions, 2011.

Bestall, Cliff, dir. "The 16th Man." *ESPN 30 for 30*. United States: ESPN, 2010.

Betkhe, Jefferson. "Why I Hate Religion, But Love Jesus." *YouTube*, January 10, 2012. https://www.youtube.com/watch?v=1IAhDGYlpqY.

Bhansali, Sanjay Leela, dir. *Black*. India: Applause Bhansali Productions, 2005.

Bidini, Dave. *Home and Away: One Author's Inspiring Experience at the Homeless World Cup*. New York: Skyhorse, 2011.

Block, Alan A. *The Classroom: Encounter and Engagement*. New York: Palgrave Macmillan, 2014.

Bobbitt, Franklin. "The Actual Objectives of the Present-Day High School." *American Journal of Education* 91.4 (August 1983) 450–67.

Bonfiglio, Michael, dir. "You Don't Know Bo: The Legend of Bo Jackson." *ESPN 30 for 30*. United States: ESPN, 2012.

Bibliography

Bosco, John. "The Preventive System in the Education of the Young." Translated by P. Laws. http://www.sdb.org.hk/dbway/source/article/article/DB%20Preventive%20 System%201877.pdf.

Boske, Christa. "Bullied: What's Going On?" In *Students, Teachers, and Leaders Addressing Bullying in Schools*, edited by Christa Boske and Azadeh Oslanoo, 1–22. Boston: Sense, 2015.

Boske, Christa, and Azadeh Oslanoo, eds. *Students, Teachers, and Leaders Addressing Bullying in Schools*. Boston: Sense, 2015.

———. "Uncomfortable Truths: An Introduction to Bullying in U.S. Schools." In *Students, Teachers, and Leaders Addressing Bullying in Schools*, edited by Christa Boske and Azadeh Osanloo, xiii–xxiii. Boston: Sense, 2015.

Brueggemann, Walter. "Covenanting as a Human Vocation: A Discussion of the Relation of Bible and Pastoral Care." *Interpretation—Journal of Bible and Theology* 33.2 (1979) 115–29.

———. *Sabbath as Resistance: Saying No to the Culture of Now*. Rev. ed. Louisville: Westminster John Knox, 2017.

Canales, Arthur David. *A Noble Quest: Cultivating Spirituality in Catholic Adolescents*. Waco: PCG Legacy, 2011.

Carey, Lamont. *Def Poetry Jam*. Episode 5, "I Can't Read." United States: HBO, 2007.

Carr, Nicholas. *The Shallows: What the Internet is Doing to Our Brains*. New York: Norton, 2011.

Catechism of the Catholic Church. 2nd revised ed. Libreria Editrice Vaticana, 2000.

Centers for Disease Control and Prevention. "Youth Risk Behavior Surveillance—United States, 2015." *Morbidity and Mortality Weekly Report* 65.6 (2015). https://www.cdc. gov/healthyyouth/data/yrbs/pdf/2015/ss6506_updated.pdf.

Convey, John J. *What Do Our Children Know About Their Faith? Results from the ACRE Assessment*. Arlington, VA: NCEA, 2010.

Convey, John J., and Andrew D. Thompson. *Weaving Christ's Seamless Garment: Assessment of Catholic Religious Education*. Washington, DC: NCEA, 1999.

Correal, Annie, et al. "March for Our Lives Highlights: Students Protesting Guns Say 'Enough is Enough.'" *The New York Times*, March 24, 2018. https://www.nytimes. com/2018/03/24/us/march-for-our-lives.html.

Couturié, Bill. "Guru of Go." *ESPN 30 for 30*. United States: ESPN, 2010.

Croghan, Richard V. "Mahanambrata Brahmachari and Thomas Merton." *The Merton Seasonal* 43.2 (2018) 3–10.

Daggy, Robert. "Editorial: Dan Walsh and Thomas Merton." *The Merton Seasonal* 5.2 (1980) 2.

———. "The Road to Joy: Thomas Merton's Letters to and about Young People." In *Toward an Integrated Humanity: Thomas Merton's Journey*, edited by M. Basil Pennington, 52–73. Kalamazoo, MI: Cistercian, 1987.

———. "Thomas Merton & the Quiz Show Scandal: 'America's Loss of Innocence.'" *The Merton Seasonal* 20.2 (1995) 4–11.

Dean, Kenda Creasy. *Almost Christian: What the Faith of Our Teenagers Is Telling the American Church*. New York: Oxford University Press, 2010.

———. *Practicing Passion: Youth and the Quest for a Passionate Church*. Grand Rapids, MI: Eerdmans, 2004.

Delgatto, Laurie, ed. *Catholic Youth Ministry: The Essential Documents*. Winona, MN: Saint Mary's, 2005.

Bibliography

Del Prete, Thomas. *Thomas Merton and the Education of the Whole Person*. Birmingham: Religious Education, 1990.

———. "Thomas Merton on Mark Van Doren: A Portrait of Teaching and Spiritual Growth." *Merton Seasonal* 16.1 (1991) 16–18.

Derrickson, Scott, dir. *Doctor Strange*. New York: Marvel Studios, 2016.

Distefano, Anthony. "Dan Walsh's Influence on the Spirituality of Thomas Merton." *The Merton Seasonal* 5.2 (1980) 4–13.

Doctrinal Elements of a Curriculum Framework for the Development of Catechetical Materials for Young People of High School Age. Washington, DC: USCCB, 2008.

Downie, Gord, and Jeff Lemire. *Secret Path*. London: Simon & Schuster, 2016.

East, Thomas, et al. *Leadership for Catholic Youth Ministry: A Comprehensive Resource*. 2nd ed. New London, CT: Twenty-Third, 2016.

Eisner, Elliot W. "Artistry in Education." *Scandinavian Journal of Educational Research* 40.3 (2003) 373–84.

———. *The Arts and the Creation of the Mind*. New Haven, CT: Yale University Press, 2004.

———. "Educating the Whole Person: Arts in the Curriculum." *Music Educators Journal* 73.8 (1987) 37–41.

———. "Educational Connoisseurship and Criticism: Their Form and Functions in Educational Evaluation." *The Journal of Aesthetic Education* 10.3/4 (1976) 135–50.

———. "Objectivity in Educational Research." *Curriculum Inquiry* 22.1 (1992) 9–15.

———. "Preparing for Today and Tomorrow." *New Needs, New Curriculum* 61.4 (2004) 6–10.

———. "Questionable Assumptions about Schooling." *Phi Delta Kappan* 84.9 (2003) 648-57.

Flinders, David A., and Elliot W. Eisner. "Educational Criticism as a Form of Qualitative Inquiry." *Research in the Teaching of English* 28.4 (1994) 341–57.

Forest, Jim. *Living with Wisdom: A Life of Thomas Merton*. Rev. ed. Maryknoll, NY: Orbis, 2008.

"Fortnite." https://en.wikipedia.org/wiki/Fortnite.

Francis, Pope. "Address of Pope Francis to Students and Teachers from Schools across Italy." http://www.vatican.va/content/francesco/en/speeches/2014/may/documents/papa-francesco_20140510_mondo-della-scuola.html.

———. "Christus Vivit." http://www.vatican.va/content/francesco/en/apost_exhortations/documents/papa-francesco_esortazione-ap_20190325_christus-vivit.html.

———. "Evangelii Gaudium." http://www.vatican.va/content/francesco/en/apost_exhortations/documents/papa-francesco_esortazione-ap_20131124_evangelii-gaudium.html.

Franklin, R. William, and Joseph M. Shaw. *The Case for Christian Humanism*. Grand Rapids, MI: Eerdmans, 1991.

Fullan, Michael. *The New Meaning of Educational Change*. 4th ed. New York: Teachers College, 2007.

Gan, Nectar, and Emiko Jozuka, "Chinese Fans in Mourning: Kobe Bryant's Death Draws an Outpouring of Shock and Grief." *CNN*, January 27, 2020. https://www.cnn.com/2020/01/27/asia/asia-mourns-kobe-bryant-intl-hnk/index.html.

Giussani, Luigi. *The Risk of Education: Discovering Our Ultimate Destiny*. Translated by Rosanna M. Giammanco Frongia. New York: The Crossroad, 2001.

Bibliography

Grayston, Donald. *Thomas Merton and the Noonday Demon: The Camaldoli Correspondence*. Eugene, OR: Cascade, 2015. Ebook.

Greenfield, Susan. *Mind Change: How Digital Technologies are Leaving Their Mark on Our Brains*. New York: Random House, 2015.

Hall, Cassidy, dir. *Day of a Stranger*. Transcendental Media, 2019.

Hehir, Jason, dir. "The '85 Bears." *ESPN 30 for 30*. United States: ESPN, 2016.

Henderson, James G., and Kathleen R. Kesson. *Curriculum Wisdom: Educational Decisions in Democratic Societies*. Upper Saddle River, NJ: Pearson, 2004.

Higgins, Michael W. *Thomas Merton: Faithful Visionary*. Collegeville, MN: Liturgical, 2014.

Hilbert, Martin, and Priscila López. "The World's Technology Capacity to Store, Communicate, and Compute Information." *Science* 332.6025 (2011) 60–65.

Horan, Daniel P. *The Franciscan Heart of Thomas Merton: A New Look at the Spiritual Inspiration of His Life, Thought, and Writing*. Notre Dame: Ave Maria, 2014.

Huggins, Michael. "Stigma Is the Origin of Bullying." *Journal of Catholic Education* 19.3 (2016) 166–96.

Huie, William Bradford. "Death of an Innocent: What Kind of Mind Could Have Planted the Bomb that Killed Four Children in Birmingham?" *LOOK*, March 24, 1964. http://sixtiessurvivors.org/ft_innocent.html.

"Investigation of Television Quiz Shows: Hearings before a Subcommittee of the Committee on Interstate and Foreign Commerce, House of Representatives, Eighty-sixth Congress, First Session." https://archive.org/stream/investigationoft01unit/investigationoft01unit_djvu.txt.

Jackson, Peter, dir. *The Lord of the Rings: The Fellowship of the Ring*. United States: New Line Productions, 2001.

Jackson, P. W. "Shifting Visions of the Curriculum: Notes on the Aging of Franklin Bobbitt." *The Elementary School Journal* 75 (1975) 118–33.

Johnson, Rhiannon. "Centre for Truth and Reconciliation to Develop Memorial Register of Residential School Deaths." *CBC News*, October 27, 2018. https://www.cbc.ca/news/indigenous/residential-school-student-memorial-register-1.4880391.

John Paul II, Pope. "Beatification Homily." https://frassatiusa.org/beatification-homily.

———. "Catechesi Tradendae." http://www.vatican.va/content/john-paul-ii/en/apost_exhortations/documents/hf_jp-ii_exh_16101979_catechesi-tradendae.html.

———. "Dilecti Amici." http://www.vatican.va/content/john-paul-ii/en/apost_letters/1985/documents/hf_jp-ii_apl_31031985_dilecti-amici.html.

———. "Jubilee of Sports People: Homily of John Paul II." http://www.vatican.va/content/john-paul-ii/en/homilies/2000/documents/hf_jp-ii_hom_20001029_jubilee-sport.html.

Joy of Adolescent Catechesis. Washington, DC: NCEA, 2017.

Kennedy, Patrick, and Andrea Prat. "Where Do People Get Their News?" *Columbia Business School Research Paper* 17-65 (2018). http://dx.doi.org/10.2139/ssrn.2989719.

Kimble, Bo. "Hank." *The Players' Tribune*, March 25, 2015. https://www.theplayerstribune.com/en-us/articles/ncaa-ournament-march-madness-loyola-marymount-bo-kimble-hank-gathers.

Kinnane, Charles Frances, dir. *The Human Experience*. United States: Grassroots Films, 2010.

Labrie, Ross. *Thomas Merton and the Inclusive Imagination*. Columbia, MO: University of Missouri Press, 2001.

Leonard, Erin. *The Battle against Juvenile Bullying: The Plague of Child and Teen Bullying in the Schools and How to Stop It.* Atlanta: Anaphora, 2014.

Leseur, Elisabeth. *My Spirit Rejoices: The Diary of a Christian Soul in an Age of Unbelief.* Manchester, NH: Sophia Institute, 1996.

———. *Selected Writings: Classics of Western Spirituality.* New York: Paulist, 2005.

Levinson-King, Robin. "Canada Reveals Names of 2,800 Victims of Residential Schools." *BBC News*, October 1, 2019. https://www.bbc.com/news/world-us-canada-49884387.

Lipsey, Roger. *Angelic Mistakes: The Art of Thomas Merton.* Brattleboro, VT: Echo Point, 2018.

———. *Make Peace Before the Sun Goes Down: The Long Encounter of Thomas Merton and His Abbot, James Fox.* Boston: Shambhala, 2015.

"Living as Missionary Disciples: National Directory for Catechesis Worksheets." Washington, DC: USCCB, 2017. http://www.usccb.org/beliefs-and-teachings/how-we-teach/catechesis/catechetical-sunday/living-disciples/upload/7-571-missionary-disciples-ndc-worksheets.pdf.

Lorenz, Taylor. "Teens Explain the World of Snapchat's Addictive Streaks, Where Friendships Live or Die." *Business Insider*, April 14, 2017. https://www.businessinsider.com/teens-explain-snapchat-streaks-why-theyre-so-addictive-and-important-to-friendships-2017-4.

Lunson, Lian, dir. *Leonard Cohen: I'm Your Man.* Sundance Channel/Horse Pictures, 2005.

Malewitz, Thomas E. "No One is an Island: Student Experiences of a Catholic High School Curriculum Response to Bullying, Based on Themes from the Writings of Thomas Merton." PhD diss., Bellarmine University, 2018. https://scholarworks.bellarmine.edu/tdc/61/.

———. "Who Am I? Why Am I Here? Revisiting Renewing the Vision and Contemporary Challenges of Catholic Adolescents—with Possible Solutions." *Momentum* 44.4 (2013) 23–25.

Malewitz, Thomas E., and Beatriz Pacheco. "Living Solidarity: Helping Students with Learning Differences Develop Dignity for All Humanity." *Journal of Catholic Education* 20.1 (2016) 324–32.

Mandela, Nelson. "Speech at the Inaugural Laureus Lifetime Achievement Award." Monaco, 2000. http://db.nelsonmandela.org/speeches/pub_view.asp?pg=item&ItemID=NMS1148&txtstr=Laureus.

Marcia, James E., et al. *Ego Identity: A Handbook for Psychological Research.* New York: Springer, 2006.

Mata, Jennifer. "Meditation: Using It in the Classroom." In *Spirituality in the 21st Century: Journeys Beyond Entrenched Boundaries*, edited by Wim Van Moer et al., 109–19. Oxford: Inter-Disciplinary, 2013.

McDonnell, Thomas P. "An Interview with Thomas Merton." *Motive* 27 (Oct 1967) 32–41.

Meatyard, Ralph Eugene. "A Eulogy of Thomas Merton." In *Father Louie: Photographs of Thomas Merton*, edited by Barry Magid, 57–58. New York: Timken, 1991.

———. *Father Louie: Photographs of Thomas Merton.* Edited by Barry Magid. New York: Timken, 1991.

Medina, Jennifer, et al. "Los Angeles Teachers Strike, Disrupting Classes for 500,000 Students" *The New York Times*, January 14, 2019. https://www.nytimes.com/2019/01/14/us/lausd-teachers-strike.html.

Mercadante, Frank. *Engaging a New Generation: A Vision for Reaching Catholic Teens.* Huntington, IN: Our Sunday Visitor, 2012.

Bibliography

Merton, Thomas. *The Asian Journals of Thomas Merton*. Edited by Naomi Burton et al. New York: New Directions, 1980.

———. "Blessed Are the Meek: The Christian Roots of Nonviolence." In *Thomas Merton On Peace*, edited by Gordon C. Zahn, 208–18. New York: McCall, 1971.

———. "Cables to the Ace #8." In *The Collected Poems of Thomas Merton*, 399–400. New York: New Directions, 1980.

———. "Christian Humanism." In *Love and Living*, edited by Naomi Burton Stone and Patrick Hart, 135–50. San Diego: Harcourt, 1979.

———. "Christian Humanism in the Nuclear Era." In *Love and Living*, edited by Naomi Burton Stone and Patrick Hart, 151–69. San Diego: Harcourt, 1979.

———. *The Collected Poems of Thomas Merton*. New York: New Directions, 1980.

———. *Conjectures of a Guilty Bystander*. New York: Image, 2009.

———. "Contemplation in a World of Action." In *Thomas Merton, Spiritual Master*, edited by Lawrence S. Cunningham, 368–87. New York: Paulist, 1965.

———. *Contemplative Prayer*. New York: Image, 2014.

———. *Faith and Violence: Christian Teaching and Christian Practice*. Notre Dame: University of Notre Dame Press, 2015.

———. "Hagia Sophia." In *The Collected Poems of Thomas Merton*, 363–71. New York: New Directions, 1980.

———. *The Hidden Ground of Love: The Letters of Thomas Merton on Religious Experience and Social Concerns*. Edited by William Shannon. New York: Farrar, Straus & Giroux, 1985.

———. "I Believe in Love." In *The Collected Poems of Thomas Merton*. Translated by William Davis, 825–26. New York: New Directions, 1980.

———. "In Silence." In *The Collected Poems of Thomas Merton*, 280–81. New York: New Directions, 1980.

———. *The Journals of Thomas Merton*. Vol. 1, *1939–1941: Run to the Mountain: The Story of a Vocation*. Edited by Patrick Hart. New York: HarperCollins, 1995.

———. *The Journals of Thomas Merton*. Vol. 2, *1941–1952: Entering the Silence: Becoming a Monk and Writer*. Edited by Jonathan Montaldo. New York: Harper Collins, 1996.

———. *The Journals of Thomas Merton*. Vol. 3, *1952–1960: A Search for Solitude: Pursuing the Monk's True Life*. Edited by Lawrence S. Cunningham. New York: HarperCollins, 1996.

———. *The Journals of Thomas Merton*. Vol. 5, *1963–1965: Dancing in the Water of Life: Seeking Peace in the Hermitage*. Edited by Robert E. Daggy. New York: HarperCollins, 1997.

———. *The Journals of Thomas Merton*. Vol. 6, *1966–1967: Learning to Love: Exploring Solitude and Freedom*. Edited by Christine M. Bochen. New York: Harper Collins, 1996.

———. "Learning to Live." In *Love and Living*, edited by Naomi B. Stone and Patrick Hart, 3–24. San Diego: Harcourt, 1969.

———. "Letter to an Innocent Bystander." In *Raids on the Unspeakable*, 53–62. New York: New Directions, 1966.

———. "Letter to Antoinette M. Costa, May 13, 1965." In *The Road to Joy: Letters to New and Old Friends*, edited by Robert E. Daggy, 335. New York: Farrar, Straus & Giroux, 1989.

————. "Letter to Besti Baeten, October 2, 1967." In *The Road to Joy: Letters to New and Old Friends*, edited by Robert E. Daggy, 358–59, New York: Farrar, Straus & Giroux, 1989.

————. "Letter to Charles Van Doren, November 7, 1959." The Thomas Merton Center. Louisville.

————. "Letter to James Forest, February 21, 1966." In *The Hidden Ground of Love: The Letters of Thomas Merton on Religious Experience and Social Concerns*, edited by William Shannon, 290–93. New York: Farrar, Straus & Giroux, 1985.

————. "Letter to Jan Boggs, February 9, 1966." In *The Road to Joy: Letters to New and Old Friends*, edited by Robert E. Daggy, 338, New York: Farrar, Straus & Giroux, 1989.

————. "Letter to Lorraine, April 17, 1964." In *Witness to Freedom*, edited by William H. Shannon, 167. New York: Farrar, Straus & Giroux, 1994.

————. "Letter to Mary Declan Martin, April 1, 1968." In *The Road to Joy: Letters to New and Old Friends*, edited by Robert E. Daggy, 364. New York: Farrar, Straus & Giroux, 1989.

————. "Letter to Sr. J. M., June 17, 1968." In *A Life in Letters: The Essential Collection*, edited by William H. Shannon and Christine M. Bochen, 11–12. Norte Dame: Ave Maria, 2008.

————. "Letter to Susan Chapulis, April 10, 1967." In *The Road to Joy: Letters to New and Old Friends*, edited by Robert E. Daggy, 350–51. New York: Farrar, Straus & Giroux, 1989.

————. "Letter to Suzanne Butorovich, July 18, 1967." In *The Road to Joy: Letters to New and Old Friends*, edited by Robert E. Daggy, 309–11. New York: Farrar, Straus & Giroux, 1989.

————. "Letter to Suzanne Butorovich, June 22, 1967." In *The Road to Joy: Letters to New and Old Friends*, edited by Robert E. Daggy, 308–9. New York: Farrar, Straus & Giroux, 1989.

————. "Letter to Tony Boyd, March 20, 1967." In *The Road to Joy: Letters to New and Old Friends*, edited by Robert E. Daggy, 346–47. New York: Farrar, Straus & Giroux, 1989.

————. *A Life in Letters: The Essential Collection*. Notre Dame: Ave Maria, 2008.

————. "Litany." In *The Collected Poems of Thomas Merton*, 724–25. New York: New Directions, 1980.

————. *The Literary Essays of Thomas Merton*. Edited by Patrick Hart. New York: New Directions. 1985.

————. *Love and Living*. Edited by Naomi B. Stone and Patrick Hart. San Diego: Harcourt, 1979.

————. "Message to Poets." In *Raids on the Unspeakable*, 155–64. New York: New Directions, 1966.

————. "Midsummer 1968 Circular Letter to Friends." In *The Road to Joy: Letters to New and Old Friends*, edited by Robert E. Daggy, 115–17. New York: Farrar, Straus & Giroux, 1989.

————. *The New Man*. New York: Farrar, Straus & Giroux, 1999.

————. *New Seeds of Contemplation*. New York: New Direction, 2007.

————. *No Man Is an Island*. San Diego: Harcourt, 1983.

————. "On Remembering Monsieur Delmas." In *The Teacher*, edited by Morris L. Ernst, 45–53. Englewood Cliffs, NJ: Prentice-Hall, 1967.

———. "Original Child Bomb." In *The Collected Poems of Thomas Merton*, 293–302. New York: New Directions, 1980.

———. "Picture of a Black Child with a White Doll." In *The Collected Poems of Thomas Merton*, 626–27. New York: New Directions, 1980.

———. "Religion and Race in the United States." In *Faith and Violence: Christian Teaching and Christian Practice*, 130–44. Notre Dame: Notre Dame, 2015.

———. *The Road to Joy: Letters to New and Old Friends*. New York: Farrar, Straus & Giroux, 1989.

———. "September 1968 Circular Letter to Friends." In *The Asian Journal of Thomas Merton*, edited by Patrick Hart, 295–96. New York: New Directions, 1975.

———. *The Seven Storey Mountain: An Autobiography of Faith*. 50th Anniversary ed. New York: Mariner, 1999.

———. *Thoughts in Solitude*. New York: Farrar, Straus & Giroux, 1958.

———. "The Time of the End Is the Time of No Room." In *Raids on the Unspeakable*, 65–78. New York: New Directions, 1966.

———. *The Wisdom of the Desert*. New York: New Direction, 1970.

———. *Witness to Freedom*. Edited by William H. Shannon. New York: Farrar, Straus & Giroux, 1994.

Michaels, Barry. *Saints for Our Times: New Novenas & Prayers*. Boston: Pauline, 2007.

Mitchell, Fritz, dir. "Brave in the Attempt." *ESPN 30 for 30 Shorts*. United States: ESPN, 2015.

Montessori, Maria. "General Notes on the Education of the Senses." In *Renewing the Mind: A Reader in the Philosophy of Catholic Education*, edited by Ryan N. S. Topping, 223–29. Washington, DC: The Catholic University of America Press, 2015.

Moses, John. *Divine Discontent: The Prophetic Voice of Thomas Merton*. London: Bloombury, 2014. Ebook.

Nash, Steve, dir. "Into the Wind." *ESPN 30 for 30*. United States: ESPN, 2010.

National Directory for Catechesis. Washington, DC: USCCB Communications, 2005.

Nolan, Christopher, dir. *The Dark Knight*. United States: Warner Brothers, 2008.

Pacheco, Beatriz. *The Rise of the Human Digital Brain: How Multidirectional Thinking is Changing the Way We Learn*. Charlotte: Information Age, 2018.

Pacheco, Beatriz, and Thomas E. Malewitz. "No Soy de Aquí ni Soy de Allá: Using Mulitple Methods to Share Stories that Address the Cultural Diaspora of American Individualism for Latino Students." In *Promoting Motivation and Learning in Contexts: Sociocultural Perspectives on Educational Interventions*, edited by Gregory A. D. Liem and Dennis M. McInerney, 345–70. Charlotte: Information Age, 2020.

Padovano, Anthony T. *The Spiritual Genius of Thomas Merton*. Cincinnati: Franciscan Media, 2014.

Palmer, Parker J. *The Courage to Teach: Exploring the Inner Landscape of a Teacher's Life*. 20th Anniversary ed. San Francisco: Wiley, 2017.

Paul VI, Pope. "Marialis Cultus." http://www.vatican.va/content/paul-vi/en/apost_exhortations/documents/hf_p-vi_exh_19740202_marialis-cultus.html.

———. "Sacrosanctum Concilium." https://www.vatican.va/archive/hist_councils/ii_vatican_council/documents/vat-ii_const_19631204_sacrosanctum-concilium_en.html.

Pinar, William F., et al. *Understanding Curriculum: An Introduction to the Study of Historical and Contemporary Curriculum Discourses*. New York: Lang, 2014.

Bibliography

Pius XII, Pope. "Musicae Sacrae." http://w2.vatican.va/content/pius-xii/en/encyclicals/documents/hf_p-xii_enc_25121955_musicae-sacrae.html.

Quinn, Brandy P. "Purposeful Explorers: Adolescents Finding Their Purposes in a Catholic High School." *Journal of Catholic Education* 21.2 (2018) 53–73.

Rembert, Ron B. "Merton on Sports and Spirituality." *The Merton Seasonal* 42.1 (2017) 18–25.

Renewing the Vision: A Framework for Catholic Youth Ministry. Washington, DC: USCCB, 1997.

Roberto, John. "History of Catholic Youth Ministry." In *Leadership for Catholic Youth Ministry: A Comprehensive Resource*, edited by Thomas East et al., 25–43. New London, CT: Twenty-Third, 2016.

Rohr, Richard, and Joseph Martos. *From Wild Man to Wise Man: Reflections on Male Spirituality*. Cincinnati: Franciscan Media, 2005.

Rosen, Christine. "Virtual Friendship and the New Narcissism." *The New Atlantis: A Journal of Technology & Society* 17 (Summer 2007) 15–31.

Sax, Leonard. *Boys Adrift: The Five Factors Driving the Growing Epidemic of Unmotivated Boys and Underachieving Young Men*. New York: Basic, 2007.

Scorsese, Martin, dir. *Silence*. United States: Paramount Pictures, 2016.

Shaffer, Susan Morris, and Linda Perlman Gordon. *Why Boys Don't Talk and Why It Matters: A Parent's Guide to Connecting with Your Teen*. New York: McGraw-Hill, 2005.

————. *Why Girls Talk and What They're Really Saying: A Parent's Guide to Connecting with Your Teen*. New York: McGraw-Hill, 2005.

Shannon, William H. *Thomas Merton: An Introduction*. Cincinnati: Franciscan Media, 2005.

Shaw, Joseph M., et al., eds. *Readings in Christian Humanism*. Minneapolis: Fortress, 2009.

Simon, Ellen. "How Instagram Makes Money." https://www.investopedia.com/articles/personal-finance/030915/how-instagram-makes-money.asp.

Smith, Christian, and Melinda Lundquist Denton. *Soul Searching: The Religious and Spiritual Lives of American Teenagers*. New York: Oxford University Press, 2005.

Spirit Juice. "Fr. Pontifex—Why I Love Religion, And Love Jesus." *YouTube*, January 19, 2012. https://www.youtube.com/watch?v=Ru_tC4fv6FE.

Stoner, Santino, dir. "Noise." *NOOMA 005*. United States: Zondervan, 2014.

Tennyson, Alfred Lord. *The Complete Alfred Lord Tennyson: The Complete Poetry and Drama*. N.p.: Bybliotech, 2015.

Tomeo, Teresa. *Noise: How our Media-Saturated Culture Dominates Lives and Dismantles Families*. West Chester, PA: Ascension, 2007.

Topping, Ryan N. S. *The Case for Catholic Education: Why Parents, Teachers, and Politicians Should Reclaim the Principles of Catholic Pedagogy*. Kettering, OH: Angelico, 2015.

Topping, Ryan, ed. *Renewing the Mind: A Reader in the Philosophy of Catholic Education*. Washington, DC: The Catholic University of America Press, 2015.

Tosun, L. Pinar. "Motives for Facebook Use and Expressing 'True Self' on the Internet." *Computers in Human Behavior* 28.4 (2012) 1510–17.

Trepany, Charles. "Rebecca Black Opens Up about Depression, Bullying She Faced for Viral Video 'Friday.'" *USA Today*, February 11, 2020. https://www.usatoday.com/story/entertainment/music/2020/02/11/rebecca-black-opens-up-life-9-years-after-friday-viral-fame/4730398002/.

Bibliography

Uhrmacher, P. Bruce, et al. *Using Educational Criticism and Connoisseurship for Qualitative Research*. New York: Routledge, 2017.

Van Doren, Charles. "All the Answers: The Quiz—Show Scandals—and the Aftermath." *The New Yorker*, July 28, 2008. https://www.newyorker.com/magazine/2008/07/28/all-the-answers.

Van Doren, Mark. *The Selected Letters of Mark Van Doren*. Edited by George Hendrick. Baton Rogue: Louisiana State University Press, 1987.

Van Thuan, Francis Xavier Nguyen. *Five Loaves & Two Fish*. Boston: Pauline, 1997.

———. *The Road of Hope: A Gospel from Prison*. Translated by John Peter Pham. North Palm Beach, FL: Wellspring, 2018.

Waldron, Robert G. *Thomas Merton—The Exquisite Risk of Love: The Chronicle of a Monastic Romance*. London: Darton, Longman & Todd, 2012.

Weakland, Rembert G. *A Pilgrim in a Pilgrim Church: Memoirs of a Catholic Archbishop*. Grand Rapids, MI: Eerdmans, 2009.

Weaver, Libby. *Exhausted to Energized*. Carlsbad, CA: HayHouse, 2018.

Weigel, George. *Witness to Hope: The Biography of Pope John Paul II*. New York: HarperCollins, 2005. Ebook.

Wiseman, Rosalind. *Queen Bees & Wannabes: Helping Your Daughter Survive Cliques, Gossip, Boyfriends, and the New Realities of Girl World*. New York: Three Rivers, 2009.

Yar, Sanam, and Jonah Engel Bromwich. "Tales from the Teenage Cancel Culture: What's Cancel Culture Really Like? Ask a Teenager. They Know." *The New York Times*, October 31, 2019. https://www.nytimes.com/2019/10/31/style/cancel-culture.html.

Zimmermann, Jens. "Introduction." In *Re-Envisioning Christian Humanism: Education and the Restoration of Humanity*, edited by Jens Zimmermann, 1–15. Oxford: Oxford University Press, 2017.

Zinger, Lana. "Educating for Tolerance and Compassion: Is There a Place for Meditation in a College Classroom?" *College Teaching Methods & Styles Journal* 4.4 (2008) 25–28.

Zipple, Jeremy, dir. *Xavier: Missionary and Saint*. United States: Janson Media, 2006.

Zoeller, Adam P., and Thomas E. Malewitz. "Tolkien's Allegory: Using Peter Jackson's Vision of Fellowship to Illuminate Male Adolescent Catholic Education." *Journal of Catholic Education* 22.1 (2019) 66–83.

Zuercher, Suzanne. *The Ground of Love and Truth: Reflections on Thomas Merton's Relationship with the Woman Known as 'M.'* Chicago: In Extenso, 2014.

———. *Merton: An Enneagram Profile*. Notre Dame: Ave Maria, 1996.

CPSIA information can be obtained
at www.ICGtesting.com
Printed in the USA
BVHW042205080820
585659BV00013B/666

9 781532 682223